Japanese and Chinese C
Begi

2 Books In 1: Learn How T̸ ̸ood At Home With 77 Easy ̸es (X2)

By

Adele Tyler

Sushi and Bento Cookbook

77 Recipes to Prepare Traditional Japanese Food At Home

By

Adele Tyler

The trademarks that are used are without any consent, and the publication of the trademark is without permission or backing by the trademark owner. All trademarks and brands within this book are for clarifying purposes only and are the owned by the owners themselves, not affiliated with this document.

Table of contents

Introduction

Sushi developed as a means of storing both rice and fish layers of rice and salmon preserved for up to months. This was the oldest forms of sushi, dating back to about the 8th century. This is much less popular now; rather than being permitted to ferment gradually, sushi rice is vinegar. Even the mixture of vinegar rice with either eggs, onions, or raw or fried fish is simply sushi. The first modern sushi is compressed, made in a storage container with a lower side of rice and an upper surface of fish and measured. Nigiri sushi was developed in the middle of the 19th century as a type of ready meals and as a consequence of rice scarcity and food shortages, gained prominence during the Second World War. Sashimi is fresh fish or brined fish without rice.

In basic words, Bento is a single-serving, prepared lunch already cooked and ready for savouring, carried by the eater. Traditionally, Bento serves as the base starch pasta or rice, followed by a nutrient or two such as fish, eggs, or beef.

With a selection of marinated and fried vegetables, and a few pieces of fruits, these two main focus points are accentuated, making a conveniently prepared meal for healthier living away from home. Advanced Bento, such as the addition of burgers, milk, dessert, green lettuce and roast potatoes, would draw influence from the western world.

Sushi has many health benefits. The salmon in sushi is cognitive food in which Omega3 fatty acids nurture, and repair brain cells to help calm the mind, sustain attention and systems performance, as fish is also highly nutritious. Fish oils could assist with more severe symptoms, such as psychosis and schizophrenia disorders, by eating rice frequently. Vitamin B12, which maintains the brain 'pleased' and staves off periods of depression, anxiousness and brain fog, is also significant in fish. Sushi is a famous and successful source of antioxidants that slows down the damage caused by cells, inhibits perpetual skin oxidative stress and slows down total ageing. These acids maintain the skin's cellular structure, help to keep cells youthful, both internal and external and are essential to anti-aging foods.

There are many types of sushi and Bento. The most common and famous types are described in the book. "Sushi and Bento Cookbook" has four chapters with all relative and vital information about sushi and Bento. Chapter one is about sushi, sushi history, sushi types, nutritional information, preparing it at home and interesting facts. Chapter two has all information about Bento, history, types, nutritional information, preparing it at home and interesting facts. Chapter three contains delicious Japanese sushi recipes. In chapter four, you will get traditional bento recipes to make your lunch colourful and flavorful. Lastly, the conclusion will give you an overview of sushi and Bento.

Chapter 1: Sushi: The Most Famous Japanese Food

Sushi is probably the world's most popular Japanese cuisine. Any meal made with vinegar rice is known as sushi. Many forms of fish are used in sushi dishes, but you can produce sushi without using any seafood or fresh fish. Because the ocean covers Japan, both seafood and rice have always been commonly eaten. Originally, sushi was preserved fish with rice stored in salt, and this became a standard dish for a thousand years in Japan before the development of modern sushi in the Edo Era. The name "sushi" means "this is sour", which represents the roots of sushi being stored in salt. To be a kind of junk food, current sushi was created and retained so to this day.

Sushi evolved by pickling it in rice as a way of storing food. Many people presume it is Japanese, but in the 2nd century AD, this was first used in China. It was not until the 8th and 9th centuries that it entered Japan.

This processed rice was initially eaten, and the fish was cooked, which became a perfect protein source, and the salmon was full of Omega-3 fats. This was the Japanese who along with rice, chose to consume the tuna, which had become seisei sushi.

In Japanese food, this modern method of eating fish was no more restoration, but the latest dish. With several new styles of sushi being developed, sushi is becoming more and more popular around the world. Sushi is a global cuisine today, with sushi restaurants and sushi fast food places all around the globe. In Japan, sushi is consumed commonly on special occasions. Sushi can currently be described as a rice-containing dish cooked with sushi vinegar.

1.1 Sushi Story

Sushi has been there, but not in its current form, for a more extended period. The fascinating story of the evolution of a basic meal is the background of sushi. In China, in the third century A.D, everything that was to become sushi was first described. Sushi initially emerged from a means of storing rice. Fish was put in rice and left to ferment, and for some time allowed a person to keep the seafood tasty. The rice was tossed away, and when necessary or desired, the fish was consumed. The process expanded across China and had found its way to Japan by the 7th century, where sushi has traditionally been a specialty. The Japanese took the thought further, as well and started consuming the rice with the tuna. The dish was initially cooked in much the same way. Nevertheless, Matsumoto Yoshi chi of Edo began mixing the rice wine vinegar with rice at the beginning of the eighteenth century, thus making his "sushi" for selling purpose.

A man named Hanaya Yohei envisioned a significant shift in the creation and distribution of his sushi in the middle of the nineteenth century.

He placed a slice of fresh seafood on top of an elongated shaped piece of processed rice, not covering the fish in rice anymore. Currently, this style is called "nigiri sushi" (finger sushi) and is now the traditional food to consume Japanese seafood. Sushi was delivered from sushi vendors on the street at the period and was supposed to be a quick or fast bite to eat during the day. This was not just the first of the true "quick sushi", eaten from the stalls, but soon became immensely popular. This form of serving sushi soon spread across Japan from his home in Tokyo, helped by the Great Kanto disaster in 1923, when many people have lost their businesses and homes and relocated from Tokyo.

The sushi shops were closed back and went inside, under more hygienic settings, during the Second World War. Afterwards, more organized dining was given (the first versions were just an indoor variant of the sushi shops) and sushi moved from "snacks" to a real eating experience. Sushi spread across the world, and with the rise of marketing seafood, Western communities increasingly embraced this unconventional form of consuming fish, often enthusiastic with something new particularly something that had developed as elegant and innovative as sushi.

Sushi, the artistic eating experience that was once exclusive to Japan, has now developed beyond conventional Japanese practices to another degree. Modern types of sushi, such as dragon rolls and the numerous lavish "fusion" designs at luxury sushi bars, have been produced by American influence. Sushi has long past, actually at least 1,900 years, but the latest version is and understandably so, popular overseas. Sushi market is only growing and appears to continue to grow. Classic sushi restaurants sit next to "fusion" cuisine and, for their purposes, both are famous. The background of sushi is far from over yet.

Los Angeles became America's first area to accept sushi effectively. In 1970, in Hollywood, the very first sushi restaurant outside small Tokyo launched and designed to cater to actors. In order to achieve American popularity, this gave sushi the final boost it required. Soon afterwards, in both Chicago and New York, many sushi restaurants opened, making the dish spread across the U.S.

Sushi changes continuously as new ingredients, processing and finishing techniques have been developed by modern top chefs. Classic nigiri sushi is still eaten in the United States, but in recent times, cut rolls covered in soy paper or seaweed have found success. Creative innovations such as sour cream, fiery mayonnaise and heavy rolls represent a distinct impact from the West, which sushi enthusiasts love and despise simultaneously. Vegans can also eat modern veggie sushi wraps.

1.2 Sushi Types

There are many types of sushi. Some of these are;

Nigiri

The oblong sushi, which implies hand-pressed sushi, the best seafood. With different toppings, nigiri can be produced and is usually served in seafood restaurants. In Japan, sushi chefs have been through rigorous preparation in order to learn how to produce nigiri sushi. Nigiri comprises of fresh fish pushed on the edge of sushi rice, finely sliced. If you cannot bring yourselves to consume it fresh, there have been some kinds of nigiri which have fried or seared seafood. Some forms of nigiri, such as eel or Kani nigiri, are covered in seaweed to give extra spice.

Nigiri is the more typical type of sushi, yet many kinds of seafood can be a perfect way to experience it. Sweet tuna, salmon, and shrimp are popular sorts of nigiri, but there are many other various types. Nigiri is commonly consumed in sections, so two pieces would probably comprise of an order. Some cafes can, however, sell dishes of 6-12 items.

Narezushi

Narezushi accurately reflects the initial sushi type and is a grain and salts preserved fish that is stored for several months before being consumed. During the fermentation, the grain is tossed aside; only the seafood is consumed.

Uramaki

Uramaki is called sushi in the Western world. Essentially, it is maki that was inside out. On the outside is the grain but on the interior is the seaweed. Like maki, uramaki will consist of almost none at all. Many "unique" rolls will be made in the form of uramaki. The Dragons Roll, Flower Roll, and Spiders Roll contain several common special rolls. Unique rolls appear to have even more than six bits on average, and also have about nine each. For chefs, it is often popular to create their unique rolls exclusive to their product or place.

Oshizushi

The definition of Oshizushi is "stretched sushi" "It is sometimes referred to as hako-sushi, meaning "pack sushi". To produce this type of sushi, a bamboo mould named an oshibako is being used. With this mould, fermented bean rice and materials are formed into a container. This is then sliced into pieces that are bite-sized and consumed with chopsticks.

Tempura Rolls

Tempura rolls are a popular item on the menu at sushi places. Essentially, grilled maki or uramaki wraps are tempura slices. In a thin mixture made from flour, liquid, and eggs, tempura itself is simply a way of fried fish or veggies.

The global love of lightly fried stuff, in other terms, has also made it to the sushi community. The most common tempura wraps out there are possibly Shrimp Tempura wraps, but some unique rolls, including Crunch Rolls, Tiger Rolls, and Dragon Rolls.

Temaki

Temaki is pleasant indeed. Although regular rolls (uramaki and maki) are formed by palm, Temaki is wrapped with the aid of a bamboo mat. Temaki is cone-shaped and bigger than the regular sushi roll, so it is shaped separately. As a result, you will probably get only one roll when you buy Temaki. Again, in certain "luxury" menu pieces, you can get three or four based on the cuisine.

Maki

Maki is wrapped sushi, and it is typically what you think about when someone suggests a tasty Japanese meal. Seaweed is wrapped into the rice and filled with seafood, vegetables, or other items. Six bits will comprise of a roll. From the average fresh fish like tuna, yellowtails, or salmon, to vegetables such as broccoli and carrots, Maki wraps will include just about everything. For non-fish foodies, some chefs may also use chicken.

Sashimi

Sashimi stands for "pierced body". Sashimi may usually be recognized or described as a cut of meat, not typically just salmon and not necessarily fresh, traditionally wrapped over a side and likely followed by one herb per chunk of perilla. Sashimi focuses on small cuts, such as tuna or salmon, of fresh fish. It is usually eaten on a plate of daikon radish and is not usually eaten with rice.

Assume a platter with diverse types of diced fresh fish when you request sashimi.

The type of dishes you order relies on how many you get. There can be about nine parts of main course sashimi, and a meal can have 16-20 pieces, and it varies upon the café.

1.3 Nutrition Facts of Sushi

For some period ago, sushi has always been at the centre of culinary, but a group of citizens are not aware of sushi nutrition facts. The good thing for many was that it is not a nutritious meal in general, because there is an option to manage your diet low in calories, even if you enjoy sushi. Although there are certainly a few calories to be gained in grains and egg, there are a variety of combinations you can take full advantage of it when it applies to sushi. Sashimi, for instance, are raw parts of fish that arrive without rice, and they are very healthy and high in nutrients. Here is some nutritional information about different kinds of sushi.

Avocado Roll

- Calories: 140
- Fats: 5.7g
- Carbohydrates: 28g
- Proteins: 2.1g

Shrimp Tempura Roll

- Calories: 508
- Fats: 21.0g
- Carbohydrates: 64g
- Proteins: 20g

Salmon and Avocado Roll

- Calories: 304
- Fats: 8.7g
- Carbohydrates: 42g
- Proteins: 13g

Tuna Roll

- Calories: 184
- Fats: 2.0g
- Carbohydrates: 27g
- Proteins: 24g

California Roll

- Calories: 255
- Fats: 7.0g
- Carbohydrates: 38g
- Proteins: 9.0g

Cucumber Roll

- Calories: 136
- Fats: 0.0g
- Carbohydrates: 30g
- Proteins: 6.0g

Spicy Tuna Roll

- Calories: 290
- Fats: 11.0g
- Carbohydrates: 26g
- Proteins: 24g

1.4 Preparing Sushi at Home

Your seafood taste is the first aspect to take into consideration. Some individuals chose to use prepared products such as eel or preserved products such as sushi rice, either because they are more familiar with prepared or processed foods, or because they are more confident with prepared or processed foods, or to prevent the risk for infection. But always have your interests in mind as well as those you are going to dine with. Raw fish is better ordered from a fishmonger or supermarket where they know the fish is supposed to be consumed raw. Some supermarkets have this greater fish easily accessible, but still, inquire if you are uncertain. Japanese supermarkets will also have seafood of sushi quality to buy. Here is some traditional and necessary equipment you need to have while preparing sushi at home.

Food Items

You would certainly not forget these, either fish, veggies, or whatever might hit your imagination, but the trick is to have them ready for usage in or on your sushi until you begin preparing. When preparing sushi, you do not need to have to slice a fillet. Once you sit down to prepare the sushi, the parts should be of sushi length. But note, first, safety is necessary. When you are about to make your sushi, keep all the fresh fish frozen and free from pollutants.

Bamboo Mat

This is used to roll and form split rolls, named maki, and if maki is made, it is essential. They are genuinely invaluable since they guarantee accuracy in the finished product, and you will be hard-pressed without one to roll anything as big without a debacle as a layer of nori (seaweed). Some protect their maki with the bamboo wrap that can make it easier to press and release the roll.

A Sharp Knife

If you do not have a good knife for the work, chopping up all the products would be more time-consuming and challenging. For slicing fish, the Japanese have produced a unique knife named a bento knife that does the work very well. However, as every sharp knife can do, there was no need to go out there and purchase one just for this function. But ensure that the knife is smooth, since the finer the knife, the smoother and more accurate the cuts you can make. Your sushi maki would be smashed by a blunt knife and must be left pretty nasty.

Sushi Rice

Rice that is well cooked and processed is essential to the process. It is also quite important to have the proper temperature for your rice. The only grain which can be used for producing sushi is simple Japanese rice; it also has the perfect amount of starch to hold it bound together to guarantee a properly finished result. .This should fit well for you if you have a slow cooker. Rice for sushi, neither heated nor cold, must be well carbonated and at ambient temperature. This way, it will have the right quality as well as the requisite sushi residue.

1.5 Interesting Facts about Sushi

Here are some interesting facts about sushi.

Sushi Originated Outside of Japan

The idea for sushi is believed to have originated in Southeast Asia, even though the Japanese get proper points for what they call sushi nowadays. Somewhere near the River, Narezushi, a preserved fish covered in sour rice, emerged before expanding to China and eventually to Japan. Hanaya Yohei developed the advanced sushi idea in Japan somewhere right at the end of the Edo period, sometime between the 19th century.

Even Fresh Sushi Is Frozen First

In the United States and Europe, food safety laws mandate that fresh fish be preserved for a certain period in order to eliminate possible flukes and worms. In Europe, fresh fish must be stored for at least 24 hours at 30 degrees Celsius. In Foreign sushi bars, even the tastiest raw fish consumed has been processed, which destroys the initial flavour and feel. Japanese sushi leaders are qualified to recognize the possible problems of the fish they buy on the market, such as deflections and worms. It will be a horrible disgrace to make consumers ill. Thus sushi kept in the refrigerator before preparation.

Puffer Fish Is the Most Dangerous Sashimi

In its organs and glands, fugu, or pufferfish, carry deadly quantities of venom. If a chef scratches one with a knife unintentionally when cooking sashimi, he might injure his client. Cooks in Japan must undertake a stringent preparation and qualification process to be qualified to work with fugu sushi.

Sushi Rice Was Never Eaten

Sour, pickling rice was bundled around aging fish only to assist in the umami a rare, sour taste creation process. When the process of fermentation was finished, the rice was eliminated, and only the fish was eaten. Fermenting rice has also served to sustain and defend fish from insects.

Maki Rolls Are a Work of Art

Besides the "California roll" trend available at every affordable sushi outlets in the West, master chefs design the products for real makizushi so that the flavour, appearance, and even shades complement each other. Also, cut into sheets, rolls are distributed such that clients can see the creative work inside.

Cheap Fast Food

For quite some time, a gold credit card was not required to eat sushi. Initially, sushi catches on as an inexpensive, fast snack to eat while watching a theatre show with your hands.

Sushi Is Eaten With the Hands

True to its roots as basic ready meals, the right way to eat sushi is with your fingertips. Usually, chopsticks can only be used for eating tempura fish pieces.

Chapter 2: Bento: Traditional Japanese Box Lunches

In Japanese tradition, Bento boxes are the traditional lunch boxes with sections prepared by Japanese women for their partners and other family members. Initially, they originated as basic meals that needed little to no assembly effort. Currently, they are an internationally common, colourful art form. A Japanese-origin singular take-out or residence dinner. It is popular in Chinese, Korean and Taiwanese cuisines beyond Japan, and also in Southeast Asian foods where the principal food is rice.

Rice or pasta with fish or beef, sometimes with pickled and fried veggies in a package can contain a typical bento. Containers vary from disposable density items to hand-crafted processes and activities. In several locations across Japan, Bento is readily accessible, including grocery stores, bento markets, train stations and grocery stores. However, for the families, kids, or themselves, Japanese households often invest energy and time on specially packed box lunches.

The Western version of lunch in a sack or plastic bag is Japanese bento. Perhaps the biggest distinction between the two types of packaged lunches is that unlike a meal eaten on a plate at the house, bento lunches are usually conveniently packed in a re-closeable plastic package such that the whole meal is ready for your pleasure. A sack meal, on the other side, is mostly a collection of lunch items packaged in individual plastic bags or storage bins that are removable or reusable and held in a sack or backpack.

2.1 Bento History

The bento box may only seem like a fashionable Japanese lunch with a cute appearance, but for decades, bento boxes were a cornerstone of Japanese culinary culture. The word "bento" comes from the term "comfortable" in Chinese, which applies to both the bento meals and the bento container itself. The bento's oldest and most fundamental version can be traced back to the time of Kamakura, while people brought fried and roasted rice in small bags to eat at the job. The traditional wooden enamelled bento boxes started to be manufactured and used during the Azuchi-Momoyama era.

Bento grew in importance and prestige over the next several hundred and fifty years and has been used not only to prepare basic lunches but became more sophisticated and beautiful. For tea providers, cinema ad breaks, journeys, entertainment, and more, specially designed bento was used. Various cookbooks devoted to how to plan, prepare and store bento for special events started being released during the Edo era.

As during Meiji Era, bento had become a favourite among primary school children and educators as well as earlier schools did not have meals. During this period, bento boxes have started being offered at railway stations.

The aluminium bento box became common during the Taishō era and was seen as both a luxurious commodity and a source of social contention. The aluminium bento box, as well as the form of bento lunch (rich, diverse foods vs plain and loosely made meals), were extremely popular. Differences in wealth were seen all too quickly, especially in schools. Food shortages also began to hit the nation, and the tradition of taking bento to school diminished after the Second World War, as schools began supplying students and staff with lunches.

In the 1980s, thanks to the advent of the oven and the dramatic growth in grocery stores, Bento recovered prominence. Many bento stores and retailers have replaced costly wood and metal containers with cheap bento boxes made of polythene. Handcrafted bento has also crafted a resurgence; they are used fairly frequently in classrooms, are still seen as a lunch box by many staff, weekend vacations by parents, school trips, and on social networks are very popular. From grocery stores to post offices to malls to stores and cafes that specialize in bento, you can locate bento almost anywhere in Japan today.

The bento box has been accessible meal during its long existence. The bento is a staple of Japanese culinary culture that has travelled across the globe to be loved by people worldwide, from very plain and utilitarian to carefully designed, cooked and arranged.

2.2 Types of Bento

Here are some specific Bentos in Japan that you can consider:

Aisai Bento

For the spouse or kids, Aisai bento is a unique lunch to be brought to school or work. Likewise, mostly during early spring, teenage people in relationships often make a homemade bento for their considerable partners.

Shiraishi-bento

Many Japanese people who are dissatisfied with their spouses' or their children's actions make it obvious as a shikaeshi-bento or "bento of retaliation", a threat written with nori plants, rice meals, pork describing filthy taste.

Chara-ben

Chara-ben or Character-bento comprises of an intricate bento in which entities, figures or pets are portrayed by various ingredients. The gibberish's original intent was to provide the kids with humorous images to engage them in nutrition. These milestones presently give rise to big tournaments where the most imaginative meals are prepared tasty and delicious.

The Eki-ben

Eki-Ben or "bento shop" is the food trays accessible at rail and subway stations, something special you claim, but they are very common, even searched after, since many cities offer local ingredients dependent on arrangements.

2.3 Nutrition Facts of Bento

Here are nutritional information of some bento box lunches.

Simple Bento

- Calories: 267
- Carbs: 9g
- Fat: 16g
- Protein: 23g

Salmon Bento

- Calories: 860
- Carbs: 0g
- Fat: 0g

- Protein: 0g

Japanese Bento

- Calories: 443
- Carbs: 40g
- Fat: 13g
- Protein: 13g

Bento Fish

- Calories: 588
- Carbs: 86g
- Fat: 19g
- Protein: 20g

Vegetable Bento

- Calories: 615
- Carbs: 88g
- Fat: 17g
- Protein: 23g

Asda Chicken Bento Box

- Calories: 267
- Carbs: 36g
- Fat: 6g
- Protein: 16g

Japanese Bento

- Calories: 469
- Carbs: 75g
- Fat: 13g

- Protein: 14g

Bento Squit Spicy

- Calories: 20
- Carbs: 3g
- Fat: 0g
- Protein: 2g

Taiko Bento

- Calories: 195
- Carbs: 20g
- Fat: 9g
- Protein: 7g

Chicken Katsu Bento Box

- Calories: 628
- Carbs: 0g
- Fat: 0g
- Protein: 0g

2.4 Preparing Bento at Home (Tips)

The thought of doing so might sound daunting if you have never tried to make your bento, but if you bear in mind the five primary quick tips for preparing a perfect lunch, you are going to be a professional in no time.

Start With the Bento Box

It can be as elegant or as plain as you want, the bento box where the meal will be ready. You can choose from a wide range of bento box models and models with varying prices, but keep in mind the below key aspects of the bento box as you pick one that fits you and the preferences.

- A fine, stable enclosable lid is in the box.

- There are dividers in the box to generate two parts, little enough as one divider or as much as three to four separators. It is also possible to pack Bento in a clear container without dividers.

- Although most bento boxes are plain, most bento box types are rectangular for both broth and soft food with different stackable components. This type of bento box could work well if you like soup or gravies.

Plan Ahead

With just a little preparation, you can learn how simple it is to cook a nutritious lunch that can be enjoyed four days a week by you and your family and children. It seems more than possible that you have a decent share of nutritious meals at your fingertips if you are still preparing your regular meals and a weekly meal schedule. As far as bento preparation is involved, you may notice that all you need to do is to make the extra component of your early dinner so that leftover food is available next day to put into your bento.

Accessories You Need

The bento boxes, including the accessories sector, is sufficiently relevant for customers to select from a wide variety of goods accessible at conventional Japanese or European stores or digitally. Included in accessories are:

- The Forks

- Utensils

- Food sections (tiny circular silicone dividers) are used to distinguish food from fruits with liquid, for instance.

- Chopsticks

- Tiny skewers or selects to collect tiny bits of food

- Elegant plastic, paper or aluminium food cups (or cooking cups) come in various shapes and sizes to hold various kinds of food.

Balance and Aesthetics

Nutrition is among the most critical elements of preparing a bento meal. With a tiny segment of dairy, add lots of fruit and vegetables, and modest quantities of protein and whole grains. The following ratios for a nutritious meal are recommended:

- 10 percent of the fruit

- 20 percent protein

- 30 percent of whole grains

- 40 percent of veggies

Pack everything tightly and securely into your bento box jar until the things for the bento were selected. Through packing these in one portion of the bento box, and the grain and proteins in another portion of the bento box, strive and divide the fruits and vegetables. To differentiate ingredients, use bento attachments and incorporate aesthetics. Remember, the closer the food goods are crammed into your bento, and the less open space there is, the more possible it is that your bento will keep its aesthetic appeal and food will remain in place smoothly.

Bento Can Have Different Food Items

Your bento lunch's quality is not restricted to Japanese items. The bento can also contain food such as burgers, rolls, noodles and vegetables. Some snack foods can also be considered, such as bread and cheese. As described, special bento boxes may also be used to pack broth and stew into a bento lunch.

2.5 Interesting Facts about Bento

If you are on a journey to consume nutritious meals or want to save a few dollar bills, all you need to turn into your routine by bringing a lunchbox filled with healthy products such as bento snack sets. There are also plenty of lunch choices, but in the end, the decision is based on character and goals. Bento meal boxes are well prepared to suit your needs, whether you like to give children a choice at lunchtime or are searching for something nutritious to enjoy at lunch. There are interesting facts that you need to know about traditional bento boxes.

1. Currently, bento means comfort and that is just what they are, a quick way to bring food for you, consisting of convenient compartments that keep your food safe and tidy.

2. There is something like bento design here in Japan, featuring intricate designs-cute, funny, or just strange. It contains some of the excellently designed pieces of bento artwork.

3. In Japan, Makunouchi Bento can be eaten in a store. These dishes, always beautiful, are presented in exquisite lacquered cases.

4. Good for healthier dining, bento boxes enable portion control due to their distinct chambers. This is perfect for those that are trying to attain their target weight or are strive to implement that they consume a healthy dinner.

5. Japanese use lunch tin. The greatest distinction is undoubted that in order to be a lunch box, a lunch box would not have to have different containers, whereas a bento box typically has at least three compartments.

Chapter 3: Delicious Japanese Sushi Recipes

Boston Roll

Cooking Time: 1 hour

Serving Size: 32 pieces

Calories: 51

Ingredients:

- ½ Cucumber

- Masago

- 10 shrimp

- ½ avocado (sliced)

- 4 tablespoons of seasoned vinegar

- Half Nori sheets

- 2 cups of (cooked) sushi rice

Method:

1. On the cutting board, put the bamboo plate and fill it with plastic wrap.

2. Consider putting the Nori sheet over the tray, having to face upward on the stiff side.

3. Grab a bunch of sushi rice and wet your fingers.

4. To create a fluffy coating, stretch it over the Nori sheet.

5. To fill the entire region, spray some Masago equitably on the rice.

6. To get the sushi rice facing downwards, switch the mat out.

7. On the Nori, align the shrimps from one finish to the other.

8. Put beside the shrimps the finely cut cucumbers.

9. Now over the shrimps, put 2 parts of avocado.

10. Spray the avocado pieces with some lime juice to help avoid them from rust coloured.

11. Slide the bamboo mat to construct a compact roll.

12. Cut it into 6-8 parts and serve with the sauce of your preference.

13. Repeat the residual ingredients steps.

Caterpillar Roll

Cooking Time: 25 minutes

Serving Size: 12

Calories: 65

Ingredients:

- Eel Sauce

- Toasted sesame seeds
- 2 cups of Sushi Rice
- Sliced cucumber
- 1 Avocado (sliced)
- 4 pieces Shrimp
- 2 sheets of Nori

Method:

1. Cut 2 parts of tempura shrimp horizontally in the quarter to make sure that the size of the Nori sheet is covered and kept aside.

2. On a working surface, put a bamboo plate and handle it with plastic wrap.

3. Put half the Nori sheet still, rough face up.

4. Take 2/3 cups of rice from the sushi and expand it over the sheet.

5. Turn over the mat to have Nori facing up instead of down.

6. Add to the core the bits of shrimp and finely cut slices of cucumber.

7. Keep the bamboo mat from the lower part and make a compact roll using your hands and wrap the corners by smearing some liquid on it.

8. Organize all the thinly chopped half avocado bits slantingly on the edge of the roll to make it look like a caterpillar and select gently using a plastic wrap.

9. With the plastic already on, soak the knife to cut out six pieces of the roll.

10. Take the plastic off now and put some eel sauce on it.

11. Serve with the gravy. Repeat the residual ingredients steps.

Sushi Roll

Cooking Time: 38 minutes

Serving Size: 8

Calories: 126

Ingredients:

- 2 avocados
- Whole sheets of Nori
- sushi-grade tuna
- 1 sushi-grade sea bass
- 2 cups of sushi rice
- 4 imitation crab sticks
- sushi-grade salmon
- 1 Japanese cucumber

Method:

1. First, by combining cooked rice, sugar, rice vinegar, you need to start preparing seasoned sushi rice.
2. Slice both sides of the Japanese cucumber apart, chop the grain and remove it.
3. Slice it out into narrow Julienne shape strips.
4. Split the avocado in the quarter, and the pit is erased. Carry a spoon and cautiously scoop it out.
5. Now, make thin avocado pieces. Sprinkle with a little lime juice to help avoid browning.
6. Hold the crabstick and remove the skin out small slices that resemble thin cheese pieces and set them aside.

7. Now, take a large knife to cut out small pieces of salmon, shrimp, and sea bass to get that contrast of colour schemes.

8. You may replace shrimp and any other type of fish for sea bass.

9. Slice the Nori sheet in the quarter. On a smooth surface, put the bamboo mat, handle it with plastic, and take half the Nori sheet on it.

10. Consider taking a moderate ball of rice and expand it to get an equal layer over the Nori sheet.

11. To make sure the sushi rice adheres to the piece of paper, press mildly.

12. Turn over the Nori and insert the cucumber slices, crab tiny pieces, and 2-3 diced avocado on the seaweed edge.

13. To create a tight tubular log, pick up the lower portion of the Nori sheet and begin rolling. Press gently and then erase the plastic wrap and mat.

14. Organize the fish pieces on the sushi rice horizontally now the first tuna, then salmon, after which sea bass, and repeat till the end is reached.

15. Take the narrow avocado pieces and put them in between the fish pieces.

16. Hold the plastic wrap now and placed it over the wrap and press down it to ensure that the toppings cling to the rice. With the plastic wrap still there, cut out six slices.

17. Now replace the plastic and end up serving the wasabi and soy sauce with the parts. Repeat the residual ingredients steps.

Spider Roll

Cooking Time: 1 hour 10 minutes

Serving Size: 8

Calories: 265

Ingredients:

- ½ cup green onions (sliced)
- 4 teaspoons sesame seeds
- 2 cups of (cooked) rice
- 4 Nori sheets
- 1 peeled avocado (slices)
- ¼ cup all-purpose flour
- 1-tablespoon butter
- 4 tablespoons rice vinegar
- ¼ teaspoon salt
- ¼ teaspoon black pepper
- 4 (cleaned) crabs

Method:

1. You have to combine cooked short-grain rice with a suitable amount of prepared rice vinegar in a cup to cook sushi rice and hold it aside.
2. Toss salt and pepper over the soft-shelled crabs. Cover with all-purpose flour and wipe off the excess mixture.
3. In a non-stick deep fryer, add the butter and place on medium-high heat.
4. Now cook the crabs mildly, for at least a few minutes, top side up.
5. Switch them over to the other direction and bake for three minutes again.

6. Let it cool again and cut each crab with both the legs connected into four parts.

7. Put the bamboo mat on the working surface and use a plastic sheet to protect it.

8. Now, place the outer edge of the Nori sheet on the sushi mat.

9. Take a ¾ cup of prepared sushi rice and cover it with wet hands over Nori.

10. Stretch the rice uniformly, leaving a border of just 2 inches at the lower end.

11. Organize four pieces of avocado and four horizontal bits of rough crab over sushi rice. Let the limbs of the crab protrude from Nori's sides.

12. Over the toppings, scatter some spring onions and sesame seeds.

13. Take the Nori sheet's lower portion closer to you and flip over the filling to produce a roll. As you keep rolling, keep pushing the mat softly.

14. Drench the knife and cut six of the sushi roll into equal parts. Present with your sauce of selection. Repeat the residual ingredients steps.

Philadelphia Roll

Cooking Time: 30 minutes

Serving Size: 4

Calories: 446

Ingredients:

- Wasabi

- Soya sauce

- 1 ½ ounce (smoked) salmon

- 2 tablespoons cream cheese
- 2 cups of (cooked) rice
- 1 sheet Nori
- ½ small cucumber
- 4 tablespoon rice vinegar

Method:

1. Take a bowl of prepared short-grained rice and combine it to create sushi rice with three tablespoons of prepared rice vinegar.

2. The cucumber is peeled, the seed is removed and cut into thin pieces for filling.

3. On a level surface, position the sushi mat and protect it with a clear plastic film.

4. With the hard side up, place the Nori sheet through it.

5. Take a moderate sushi rice ball and scatter it over the sheet of seaweed.

6. Moisten your hands and push gently to make sure the rice is stretched out and sticking to the sheet of Nori. Keep a 1½ -inch gap at the edge, remember.

7. To bring the sushi rice out and the Nori sheet faced upward, turn over the Nori sheet.

8. On the Nori plate, smear some sour cream third up from the lower side.

9. Pick and roll small pieces of smoked salmon, and put them on the cream cheese.

10. Lay the slices of the cucumber next to it. Grab the lower part of the sushi mat and add steady pressure to get a strong log to begin rolling.

11. Moist the knife and cut out identical bits of the roll of sushi.

12. Serve with wasabi and soya sauce on a Philadelphia sushi roll. Complete the residual ingredients steps.

California Rolls

Cooking Time: 2 hours 5 minutes

Serving Size: 4 cups

Calories: 43

Ingredients:

- Wasabi
- Soy sauce
- 2 cups of (cooked) sushi rice
- 1 half cucumber (strips)
- 4 crabsticks (pieces)
- ¼ cup of rice vinegar
- 4 sheets Nori
- 1/3 cup sesame seeds
- 1 avocado (sliced)
- Juice of ½ lemon

Method:

1. If you do not plan to eat it instantly, splash lime juice on the avocado slices. This would be to prevent them from changing their shade.

2. Place and hold aside the sushi rice and now the prepared rice vinegar.

3. On an even working surface, put the bamboo mat and protect it with plastic wrap.

4. Place the Nori sheet, glossy face down, on the bamboo mat.

5. Pick and scatter a handful of sushi rice on Nori, creating an even surface.

6. To cover the area fully, spray the toasted sesame seeds over the rice.

7. To get the rice side down and Nori on edge, turn the Nori inside out.

8. In the middle portion of the Nori mat, place the pieces of avocado, cucumber and crab sticks.

9. Hold the top of the mat near you and begin rolling, holding the fillings in place to make a quick roll.

10. Humidify the knife to cut eight parts of the roll.

11. Offer with soya sauce and wasabi. Repeat the residual ingredients method.

Inari Sushi

Cooking Time: 30 minutes

Serving Size: 12

Calories: 102

Ingredients:

- 2 sheets Korean seaweed laver
- 10 square inari tofu pockets
- 4 tablespoons of rice vinegar
- 2 cups of rice

Method:

1. In a rice cooker or a pan, you have to prepare short-grained rice immediately.

2. Fluff this with a tablespoon whenever the rice is cooked well and not soggy, and let it stay for fifteen minutes.

3. Combine the rice vinegar and the sugar in a dish. Keep stirring until it fully dissolves the sugar solutes.

4. To let it settle, move the hot rice to a huge wooden pot. Transfer the vinegar-sugar spice to the rice once chilled.

5. Now, bring the crumbled laver of Korean seaweed and combine it with the seasoned rice for sushi.

6. Break the pieces of the tofu in the quarter and keep them aside.

7. Humidify your hands and render the sushi rice into twenty equal portions.

8. Offer an oval shape to each rice section and push it tightly inside the pockets of the inari.

9. Serve with sesame oil and wasabi. Repeat the residual ingredients steps.

Temaki Sushi

Cooking Time: 10 minutes

Serving Size: 2

Calories: 150

Ingredients:

- Green shiso
- Japanese Mayonnaise
- 2 cups of (cooked) sushi rice
- Ikura (Roe)
- Kaiware sprouts

- Lettuce
- Sushi- grade Tuna
- ¼ cup of rice vinegar
- Sushi-grade Salmon
- 4-5 Nori sheets

Method:

1. To obtain well-seasoned sushi rice, combine the cooked rice with prepared rice vinegar.
2. Rather than the sashimi-style, grab pieces of raw fish cuts and slice them into big sticks.
3. You do not need any bamboo mats for this dish. So, place the Nori sheet immediately, raw side up, on the workpiece.
4. Take a spoonful of sushi rice and scatter only half a portion of the Nori on the left side.
5. Now insert the fillings vertically around the centre of the sushi rice (salmon sticks, spinach, shiso, roe, kaiware sprouts, and mayonnaise). Put more fillings at the end.
6. Begin rolling from the lower left end to make a cone and go up the side.
7. To close the sides and maintain the cone, take several grains of sushi rice.
8. Serve with sesame oil and wasabi. Repeat the residual ingredients steps.

Dragon Roll

Cooking Time: 1 hour

Serving Size: 4

Calories: 454.6

Ingredients:

- 8 pieces of shrimp tempura
- 2 tablespoon Tobiko
- 1 Japanese cucumber
- 2 Nori sheets
- 2 cups of sushi rice
- 2 Avocados
- ½ lemon

Method:

1. Cut the avocado layer, break it into two halves and remove the core. Now, create and hold aside small pieces of both halves.

2. Spray the avocado pieces with some lime juice to keep them from becoming dark.

3. On a plain board, place the bamboo mat on and protect it with plastic wrap.

4. Place the half sheet of Nori, the glossy side facing downwards.

5. On the Nori mat, take a moderate ball of prepared sushi rice and make an even surface. Gently press.

6. Switch over the Nori sheet and transfer to the lower half of the Nori sheet the cucumber pieces, tempura, and tobiko.

7. To create a smooth roll, begin rolling from the lower end by pushing gently.

8. When you hit the end of the Nori mat, keep rolling. By spraying some water on it, cover the corners.

9. Put the pieces of avocado on board of the roll that covers the entire layer.

10. To pinch the roll softly, use a bamboo mat, so the avocado pieces remain around the sushi rice.

11. Wet your knife and cut out eight bits. Then use the bamboo mat to firmly grip the roll again when the roll gets rough after the cut.

12. Take the plastic wrap off now and prepare with sauce.

13. Decorate the tobiko, hot mayo, and dark sesame seeds with the dragon sushi roll.

14. Complete the residual ingredients steps.

Tiger Roll Sushi

Cooking Time: 50 minutes

Serving Size: 4

Calories: 572.9

Ingredients:

- 1 avocado (strips)
- ½ cucumber (strips)
- 250g Japanese short-grained rice
- 4 sheets Nori
- 8 leaves of baby gem lettuce
- 4 tablespoon rice vinegar
- 2 tablespoon roe
- 4 tablespoon Japanese mayonnaise
- 8 large tiger prawns

Method:

1. Firstly, seasoned sushi rice needs to be cooked.

2. To guarantee that they have been flat instead of being twisted up, loop a toothpick through the prawns.

3. Now warm the grill pan and cook the prawns, rotating them once in between for four hours. Adjust and then let chill from the heat.

4. Combine the roe and mayo. Set aside

5. Put the bamboo mat on the surface of the workpiece and use a thin plastic cover to protect it. With the thick side up, place Nori over the plastic wrap.

6. Pick a moderate sushi rice ball and scatter it to make an even surface over the Nori mat. Without squeezing, push softly.

7. Put two prawns sideways on the Nori sheet's lower end. Let part of the tail stick leftwards.

8. Place over the prawns' two baby gem leaves. Insert a couple of the cucumber and avocado pieces.

9. Over the toppings, insert a spoon of tobiko mayonnaise combination.

10. Then roll the bamboo mat with the moist hands to make a small log and cover the corners.

11. Humidify the knife and slit the ends. Now, slice each roll into three parts of equal weight.

12. Serve these bits with tasty sauces. Repeat the residual ingredients steps.

Yellowtail Sushi Roll

Cooking Time: 30 minutes

Serving Size: 2

Calories: 245

Ingredients:

- ¼ mini cucumber
- Wasabi
- 4 oz. Hamachi yellowtail
- ½ sheet nori
- 2 green onion
- ½ cup (cooked) sushi rice
- 1 teaspoon Sriracha sauce
- 1 ½ tablespoon spicy mayo
- ¼ cup vinegar

Method:

1. In a cup, combine the seasoned vinegar with the cooked sushi rice and hold it apart.

2. Make small sashimi pieces of the Hamachi yellowtail to place and hold aside over the sushi roll.

3. Slice the delicate and green section of the spring onion precisely. The cucumber is also sliced into small strips of matchbox-size.

4. The remaining portion of Hamachi is now thinly minced, but ensure you do not grind it to preserve the flavour.

5. In order to make fillings for sushi, take a very small pot and combine diced Hamachi, minced scallion, Sriracha sauce, and hot mayo.

6. Put the bamboo mat on a simple work surface and protect it with a wrap of plastic. Place the sheet of Nori on front of it.

7. Grab a handful of sushi rice and wet your palms. Place it to create an even surface over the Nori sheet.

8. Switch over the Nori so that on the plastic wrap, the rice coating faces away.

9. Now transfer the fillings to the Nori with a spoonful. Organize several cucumber bits on the Nori as well.

10. Now, begin rolling with the aid of the bamboo mat to build a compact tube. To ensure all the fillings remain intact, gently press.

11. By spraying a little water on it, keep on rolling till you hit the end and secure the sides. Erase the plastic and mat.

12. To give the added flavour and act as a gluing fluid for the fish, squeeze the spicy mayo on the rolls in a single direction.

13. Next to the line produced with spicy mayo, spill some wasabi.

14. Organize the Hamachi thinly chopped over the roll then.

15. To bring your roll a nice shape, put the plastic wrap on top of it and push firmly for a couple of seconds.

16. With the plastic wrap still being on, wet the knife to cut the sushi roll into eight bits.

17. Individually, unwrap each part and eat with soy sauce. Follow the residual ingredients steps.

Cucumber Roll

Cooking Time: 20 minutes

Serving Size: 4

Calories: 372

Ingredients:

- 4 sheets of Nori

- 2 Japanese cucumbers
- ¼ cup of rice vinegar
- 2 cups of (cooked) sushi rice

Method:

1. Mix the prepared vinegar with the cooked sushi rice to make the sushi rice.
2. Break the cucumber from both sides and remove it. Then, slice the cucumber down the middle in half. Break them in half once again to get four bits.
3. Remove the seeds and slice the cucumber parts for the sushi with julienne.
4. On an even surface, position the bamboo sheet. To avoid the mat from being dusty, protect it with a thin layer of plastic wrap.
5. Place half the sheet of Nori on the bamboo mat.
6. Take approximately ¾ cup of prepared sushi rice and scatter it to make an even coating over the Nori surface.
7. Now place the cucumber pieces on the sushi rice sideways,
8. In order to get a solid and comfortable roll, begin rolling with the bamboo mat, adding steady pressure.
9. Break 6-8 bits out of the roll and eat with wasabi and soy sauce. Follow the residual ingredients steps.

Futomaki Sushi Rolls

Cooking Time: 2 hours 45 mins

Serving Size: 4

Calories: 64

Ingredients:

Preparing Daikon Radish

- 1 tablespoon mirin
- 3 tablespoon soy sauce
- 2/3 cup dashi soup stock
- 2 tablespoon sugar
- 1-ounce daikon radish (dried)
- Water (for soaking)

Preparing Egg Omelet

- Canola oil
- 2 teaspoon sugar
- 2 eggs

Futomaki Rolls

- 4 tablespoons of vinegar
- 1 small cucumber (cut lengthwise)
- 2 cups of (cooked) Japanese rice
- 4 sheets of Nori

Method:

1. Balance cooked short-grained rice with prepared vinegar to make flavoured sushi rice.
2. Put all the ingredients in a bowl to create Kanpyo. Rinse the radish with dried daikon and drain in freshwater till smooth.
3. Squeeze excess water and cut 8-inch long strips.
4. Combine in a cup with dashi creamy soups, sugar, soy sauce, and mirin, bring to the boil and cook until the liquid disappears. Let it cool down.

5. Beat the eggs and sugars in a cup to prepare Tamagoyaki. In a bowl, heat the olive oil and add egg combination to form a layer.

6. To produce a dense roll, flip or roll the eggs omelette. Enable it to settle, then slice it into big sticks.

7. Put the sushi mat and protect it with plastic wrap on the cutting board. Place on the mat an entire sheet of dry and roasted Nori sheets.

8. Take a small ball of rice and scatter it out uniformly over the sheet of dry Nori.

9. Position the kanpyo, omelette, and cucumber pieces in the centre portion sideways.

10. Take the bamboo mat from your side, put steady pressure as you move to get a compact cylindrical tube, and begin rolling it.

11. Drench the knife and cut four bits of the rolled futomaki sushi.

12. Represent with delicious soya sauce. Follow the residual ingredients steps.

Spicy Tuna Rolls

Cooking Time: 30 minutes

Serving Size: 2

Calories: 290

Ingredients:

- ¼ cup of seasoned rice vinegar
- 2 cups (cooked) sushi rice
- 4 sheets of Nori

For Fillings

- 1 ½ tablespoon Sriracha

- 1 (sliced) green onion
- 1 ½ tablespoon mayonnaise
- 1 can (drained) tuna

Method:

1. Mix the rice vinegar with both the cooked sushi rice and hold it aside.

2. Place the bamboo mat on a smooth work surface and place one sheet of Nori above it, hard side up.

3. Take a small cup and put all the tuna mixing ingredients together and put down.

4. Humidify your hands and grab a handful of rice. Build an even surface of rice on the layer of Nori

5. Place the tuna fillings at the base of the Nori sheet then.

6. Now, take the bamboo mat and turn it to create a compact log over the lining.

7. To guarantee the roll is securely made, gently press. To cover the edges, wet your hands and tape them to the sides.

8. Moist your knife and cut it into 6-8 sizes of the same roll.

9. Present with soya sauce and wasabi. Complete the residual ingredients steps.

Traditional Sushi Rolls

Cooking Time: 1 hour

Serving Size: 10

Calories: 350

Ingredients:

- 4 tablespoon rice vinegar

- 2 cups of Japanese rice

For Fillings

- Soy sauce
- Wasabi
- 1 Japanese cucumber
- 1 tablespoon rice vinegar
- 5 Nori sheets
- 200 grams sushi-grade tuna

Method:

1. Mix the cooked short-grain rice with the prepared vinegar to make the sushi rice.
2. Break the cucumber from both sides and slice it. Now cut it straight in half and repeat to obtain four strips.
3. To get eight bits in all, remove the seeds and slice again.
4. Take out small pieces, around ¼-½ inches thick, of fresh tuna. Make the strips long.
5. On a level surface, position the bamboo mat and protect it with a sheet of plastic.
6. Place the Nori sheet on the bamboo mat then. Know that you should face the outer edge of the Nori.
7. Humidify your palms. In your hands, take a moderate ball of sushi rice and distribute an even surface on the Nori. To create steady pressure, use your hands and keep a half-inch gap on all sides.
8. Now apply to the middle portion of the rice, the cucumber and tuna pieces. You may add additional parts lined up and cover the Nori sheet's width if the tuna or cucumber parts are small.

9. To make a strong and compact block, roll the bamboo mat back from you.

10. To guarantee that the ingredients stay properly intact, continue to press gently as you roll.

11. On the sides, add a couple of drops of water and secure it. Humidify the knife and cut 6-8 parts of the roll.

12. Use soy sauce and wasabi to eat. Complete the residual ingredients steps.

Homemade Vegan Sushi Recipes

Cooking Time: 50 minutes

Serving Size: 4

Calories: 278

Ingredients:

- 1 tablespoon sugar
- 1 teaspoon of sea salt
- 4 Seaweed
- 4 cups cooked sushi rice
- 2 tablespoons rice vinegar
- Sliced cucumber

Raw Filling

- 6 sliced carrot
- 6 sliced green onion
- 6 slices cucumber
- 6 slices avocado

Cooked Filling

- 1 tablespoon Tamari soy sauce

- 1 cup sweet potato
- 1 cup Shitake mushrooms

Serving Suggestions

- Fresh pickled ginger
- Creamy peanut sauce
- Wasabi
- Tamari soy sauce

Method:

1. In a cup, add the vinegar, salt and sugar, and steam in the oven or microwave until the sugar has melted.
2. For the cooked rice, add the combination and blend well.
3. By spilling the tamari over them while enabling them to simmer a bit as you prepare the remainder of the roll ingredients and make the brined sweet potato and mushroom.
4. For 20-30 minutes, cook at 400 degrees until crispy on the sides. Until fluffy and boiled through, you can also marinate them in a bowl.
5. Place one cup of rice onto the nori sheet to start building up.
6. In a fine line, the filling components of selection lay on one side. For every filling element, you need around 2-4 bits.
7. Do not use more than four or five ingredients for fillings, or it will become too large to roll.
8. Roll firmly and cut. Serve with spices such as Tamari for dips.

Avocado Sushi

Cooking Time: 1 hour

Serving Size: 6

Calories: 140

Ingredients:

- 6 sheets (toasted) Nori
- Soy sauce, for serving
- 2 cups white rice
- 1 avocado (sliced)
- 1 tablespoon (toasted) sesame seeds
- ½ teaspoon sesame oil
- ¼ cup mayonnaise
- 3-inch piece ginger (peeled)
- 1 cup of rice wine vinegar
- 2 mini cucumbers
- 2 carrots
- 2 tablespoons sugar
- Kosher salt

Method:

1. Rinse the rice with different water adjustments, scuffling the rice with your fingers, until the water is clear.

2. Set a strainer over a basin to drain while the rest of the products are prepared.

3. Cut ginger finely along the grain into paper-thin pieces (to produce half a cup) and use a mandolin or a carrot peeler.

4. Carry a small amount of water to a boil for five seconds and add ginger. Put ¾ cup vinegar, 2 tablespoons glucose and 2 tablespoons liquid and return the pot to the burner. With salt, spray slightly.

5. Bring it to a boil, stirring until the sugar dissolves. Reserve quarter the mixture of vinegar (this would be used to spice your rice); apply the remaining vinegar to the sautéed ginger.

6. In a shallow dish, add rice and 2½ cups of water. Bring it to a simmer, then lower the temperature and cover to the lowest heat.

7. Cook for about twelve minutes until the rice is soft and all the liquid has been absorbed.

8. Withdraw from the heat. Let the lid remain on for another ten minutes. Place the rice in a wide bowl; cool for five minutes.

9. Fold with a large spatula or plastic bench sharpener in one-fourth of the allocated vinegar combination, fanning the rice when folding in the vinegar mixer to cool it down rapidly.

10. Shield with a clean kitchen towel. For assembly, reserve the remaining vinegar combination.

11. Toss the additional ¼ cup of vinegar, 1 teaspoon of sugar, a dash of salt and sesame oil with the cucumbers and vegetables while the rice is cooking.

12. Put 1 sheet of Nori, flat side down, on a rolling bamboo mat with the large side nearest to you for assembly.

13. Dampen palms with a reserve solution of vinegar and press down ¾ cup of rice evenly over Nori, leaving both sides with a ½ inch edge.

14. Spread two tablespoons of mayonnaise uniformly around the rice core. Layer ¼ cup of vegetable solution equally around the centre of the rice with a few pieces of avocado. Sprinkle the seeds of sesame.

15. Use this mat to roll the bottom third towards the middle, pressing uniformly around the roll to compact the filled, begin with the surface nearest to you.

16. Repeat with a new turn and click again softly. Remove the mat. Moist a sharp knife with a vinegar solution gently and cut into six equal parts.

17. Repeat with remaining nori covers. Use preserved pickled ginger and sesame oil to serve.

Veggie Sushi Bowls

Cooking Time: 55 minutes

Serving Size: 4

Calories: 596

Ingredients:

Rice and Seasonings

- 1 tablespoon sugar
- ½ teaspoon salt
- 2 cups of rice
- 3 tablespoons rice vinegar
- 1 ½ teaspoons tamari
- 1 sheet (dried) nori

Everything Else

- 1 avocado (sliced)
- 1 small cucumber
- 2 large carrots (sliced)

- 2 cups frozen edamame

Spicy Mayo Sauce

- ⅓ cup mayonnaise
- 2 tablespoons Sriracha

Recommended Garnishes

- Pickled ginger
- Sesame seeds

Method:

1. Bring a big pot of water on the stove for the rice to prepare. Load in the rinsed rice when the water boils and give this a mix.

2. For thirty minutes, cook the rice, then turn the heat off and rinse the rice. Put the rice back in the saucepan and cover the pot.

3. For ten minutes, just let rice heat. With a spoon, open the cover and fluff the rice.

4. To make the rice spices: Mix the tamari, rice vinegar, salt and sugar in a medium saucepan over medium heat.

5. Heat the mixture until the sugar is dissolved, stirring regularly. Remove from the heat and mix with the rice once steaming has stopped.

6. To cook the Nori: Heat the nori sheet in a frying pan over medium heat until it becomes crispy enough to crumble, flipping halfway for around five minutes quickly.

7. Rip it into pieces and extract it from the heat. In your palms, crumble each part into very tiny chunks over the rice and throw it into the bowl.

8. To cool, mix the Nori into the grain and put the rice back.

9. Take a bowl of water to a boil, then insert the freezing edamame and simmer till the beans are heated through about five minutes.

10. To prepare the edamame: Drain away and set it aside.

11. Mix all the mayonnaise and Sriracha in a shallow saucepan until well combined, to make the hot mayo sauce.

12. If you wish for a spicier sauce, put more Sriracha.

13. Cut it lengthwise in the quarter to cook the cucumber. Scoop out the seeds using a spoon and dump them.

14. Then cut the halves into bits that are two inches long and cut them into toothpicks.

15. Divide into four bowls of rice. Cover with vegetables, edamame, avocado and cucumber.

16. Sprinkle on edge with chilli-mayo sauce, scatter with sesame seeds and add on the sides with pickled ginger.

Rainbow Sushi

Cooking Time: 40 minutes

Serving Size: 4

Calories: 83

Ingredients:

- 4 tablespoon Rice vinegar
- Agave nectar
- 2 cups of cooked rice

- Sesame seeds
- Hoisin sauce
- 1 Avocado (sliced)
- 12 sheets Nori seaweed
- 1 cup cucumber (Sliced)
- ¾ cup carrots (Sliced)
- 1 cup red pepper (Sliced)
- ½ cup or shredded beets (Sliced)

Method:

1. Thinly slice the veggies or shred them. Optional: With 2-4 tablespoons of rice vinegar and several amounts of agave, spice the cooked rice.
2. Place on tops of each nori sheet with cooked rice.
3. Top with vegetables and avocado, with spraying of sesame seeds if used.
4. Roll it firmly into a log form and repeat. Break the rolls of Nori into smaller pieces. If needed, dilute the hoisin sauce with liquid for a dipping sauce.

Kid-Friendly Sushi Rolls

Cooking Time: 1 hour

Serving Size: 15

Calories: 212

Ingredients:

For the Sushi Rice

- 1 teaspoon of sea salt

- 2 cups Japanese short-grain rice

For the Filling

- 1 red bell pepper (sliced)
- 4-ounce packet smoked salmon
- ¼ cup sesame seeds
- 1 cucumber (sliced)
- 1 cooked sweet potato

Hand-Dipping Water

- 1 tablespoon vinegar
- ¼ cup of water

Everything Else

- Soy sauce for serving
- 5 sheets Nori (seaweed)

Method:

1. Either in a rice cooker or bowl, follow directions on the rice packaging to prepare your rice.

2. By mixing water and vinegar in a small cup, render the hand-dipping liquid. With this liquid, cover your hands to keep the rice from binding.

3. On a sheet lined with parchment paper, put the nori cover, with the Nori's widest side nearest to you.

4. Wet your hands with the vinegar liquid or the inside of a 1-cup mixing bowl.

5. Squeeze into your hands a meagre half a cup of sushi rice. Put and scatter the rice on the Nori, allowing one inch or two along the upper portion of the Nori.

6. If the rice begins to stick, wet your hands in the vinegar liquid. Mix rice with your wet hands slightly to coat with vinegar.

7. Spray uniformly with the sesame oil over the rice. Then in the centre of the rice, put the filling. Every component should be in line.

8. Turn the Nori across each component in one swift motion before you settle near the edge of the rice.

9. Softly form and stretch the roll into a squared or round with the parchment paper always around the roll.

10. Finally cut the parchment paper and use the water-vinegar solution to cover the surface of the Nori. Only one more time, pinch and adjust the roll.

11. Moist your knife underwater flow or with a washcloth in order to cut the sushi roll.

12. Cut rolls into small pieces and serve.

Chicken Sushi

Cooking Time: 20 minutes

Serving Size: 8

Calories: 173

Ingredients:

- 1 avocado (chopped)
- 1 small carrot (strips)
- 1½ cups of sushi rice
- 1 bamboo sushi mat
- 160g can chicken
- ½ teaspoon salt
- 4 nori sheets

- soy sauce to serve
- 3 tablespoon sushi vinegar
- wasabi to serve
- pickled ginger to serve

Method:

1. In a strainer, put the rice and thoroughly rinse under cold water.

2. Put 2½ cups of ice water and a half teaspoon of salt in a frying pan. Just bring it to a boil.

3. Allow for twelve minutes and steam. Turn off the heat and remain with the lid on for ten minutes.

4. Mix the sushi vinegar cautiously and move it to a cooling tray.

5. On a bamboo sushi mat, put a sheet of Nori, glossy side down, with the rows flowing sideways.

6. Spread about two handfuls of rice over the Nori with greasy fingers.

7. In the centre of the rice, put shredded chickens with Lite Mayo and place avocado and vegetable slices on top.

8. Pull the sushi back from you to seal the stuffing securely, and use the bamboo mat as a guideline.

9. For thirty minutes, roll in cling film and wait. With the rest of the ingredients, replicate.

10. Use wasabi, pickled ginger and sesame oil to eat.

Chapter 4: Traditional Bento Recipes

Chicken Meatball Bento

Cooking Time: 18 minutes

Serving Size: 1

Calories: 178.4

Ingredients:

- Strawberries
- Mandarin orange
- Japanese short-grain rice (Cooked)
- Japanese crab salad
- Teriyaki chicken meatballs
- Broccoli
- Cherry tomatoes
- Hard-boiled egg
- Ham Flower

Method:

1. Load ½ of the bento box with steamed rice and leave to cool.

2. Heat Teriyaki Chicken Meatballs in a deep fryer until cooked.

3. Move them and then let them cool on a small dish.

4. In the meantime, create and set aside the Ham Flower.

5. Load all the items into the bento box whenever the rice and meatballs are cold.

6. Before shutting the bento box, cool down entirely.

Sanshoku Bento

Cooking Time: 15 minutes

Serving Size: 1

Calories: 590

Ingredients:

- Shredded nori seaweed
- Strawberries
- Salted Salmon
- Roasted Chicken

Method:

1. Load rice in two - thirds of the bento box and cover the rice with salmon flakes and scrambled eggs.

2. Add roasted chicken, crushed nori and scatter in line.

3. Cover three - fourths of the bento with strawberries.

4. Before shutting the bento box, cool down entirely.

Hamburger Steak Bento

Cooking Time: 15 minutes

Serving Size: 1

Calories: 748

Ingredients:

- Corn (Cooked)
- Furikake (rice seasoning)
- Japanese short-grain rice (cooked)
- Tomato
- Celery
- Broccoli (Pre-blanched)
- Hamburger Steak

Method:

1. Load the Japanese rice in the quarter of the bento box.
2. Let it cool so that another cool item is not warmed up by hot rice.
3. In a deep fryer, reheat the leftover hamburger meat until completely hot.
4. In a silicone container, pack chilled Hamburger Steak and placed it in a bento box.
5. In the bento box, put the tomato, broccoli, celery and grain.
6. Spray on top of the rice with furikake.
7. Before locking the bento box, cool down immediately.

Asparagus Beef Roll Bento

Cooking Time: 20 minutes

Serving Size: 1

Calories: 352.7

Ingredients:

- Grapes
- Cherry tomatoes
- Edamame
- Oranges
- Onigiri (Rice Ball)
- Asparagus Beef Rolls

Method:

1. Start making Onigiri and let it cool.
2. In a deep fryer, reheat the asparagus steak rolls.
3. To let it cool, set that aside.
4. In compliance with the product instructions, cook edamame.
5. To let it cool, set it aside.
6. Slice the oranges and wash the grapes and cherry tomatoes into tiny chunks.
7. Wait for all the items to cool, then load it nicely into the bento box.
8. When locking the bento box, ensure that all the food is thoroughly cooled down.

Tempura Bento

Cooking Time: 15 minutes

Serving Size: 1

Calories: 570

Ingredients:

- Raspberries

- Grapes
- Shrimp Tempura
- Japanese short-grain rice (cooked)
- Kiwi
- Tempura dipping sauce
- Vegetable Tempura

Method:

1. Heat the tempura till it is cooked in the toaster. Set it aside to chill.
2. Load it with rice and let it cool.
3. Wash the fruits and cut them if desired.
4. Start loading cooled food in a bento box.
5. When covering the bento box, cool down food properly.

Shio Koji Karaage Bento

Cooking Time: 15 minutes

Serving Size: 1

Calories: 480

Ingredients:

- Spinach Gomaae
- furikake (rice seasoning)
- Grape tomatoes
- Tamagoyaki
- Japanese short-grain rice (cooked)
- Shio Koji Karaage

Method:

1. Load half of the bento box with steamed rice and then let it cool.

2. In the oven toaster, heat it Shio Koji Karaage until fluffy outside and hot throughout.

3. Make fast and simple Tamagoyaki, meantime, and then let it cool.

4. Place them in a bento box alongside cherry tomatoes and Tamagoyaki once Karaage and Spinach Gomaae cool down.

5. Spray on top of the rice with furikake.

6. Before shutting the bento box, cool down entirely.

Honey Soy Sauce Chicken Bento

Cooking Time: 20 minutes

Serving Size: 1

Calories: 144

Ingredients:

- Plums
- Grapes
- Onigiri (rice ball)
- Grape tomatoes
- Blueberries
- Honey soy sauce chicken
- Kosher salt
- Fresh black pepper
- tamagoyaki (1 egg + 1 teaspoon sugar)

- Cabbage (shredded)

Method:

1. Make and let the Onigiri cool.

2. Create some Tamagoyakiaki.

3. Heat the oil to fry chopped cabbage in the same frying saucepan.

4. With salt and black pepper, spray. Move to a cup of silicon.

5. Heat it the remaining honey soy sauce chicken in the same skillet until it becomes thoroughly hot.

6. Clean the mini-tomato and fruits and if appropriate, slice them.

7. Begin putting cooled food in a bento box.

8. Before shutting the bento box, cool down entirely.

Turkey Havarti Bagel Sandwich

Cooking Time: 5 minutes

Serving Size: 1

Calories: 740

Ingredients:

- 3 slices tomato
- Salt and black pepper
- 2 slices deli turkey
- Leaf lettuce
- 1 wheat bagel (sliced)
- 1 slice Cheese
- Mustard or mayonnaise

Method:

1. If needed, spread the cut side of the bagel with mayonnaise or mustard.

2. With Havarti cheese, ham, broccoli, and tomatoes, top one-third of the bagel.

3. Sprinkle with salt and peppers.

4. The other quarter of the bagel is inserted and cut in half.

5. Put in a bento box and serve.

Onigirazu

Cooking Time: 10 minutes

Serving Size: 2

Calories: 316

Ingredients:

- 1 serve Teriyaki chicken
- 1 cup Green salad leaves
- 1 piece of Tonkatsu
- 2 nori seaweed sheets
- 2 bowls (cooked) rice

Method:

1. Side to side applies to cling wrap to a cutting board or kitchen table.

2. Diagonally position one nori sheet across the clinging wrap.

3. Placed half of the rice in the middle of a sheet of nori.

4. Place the lettuce leaves on top of the rice and then a slice of tonkatsu.

5. Place over the miso katsu paste and cover with another quarter of the rice.

6. Fold the middle of all four corners of the nori sheet and cover it with the clinging wrap.

7. Set down the teriyaki chicken for several moments and replicate the same procedure.

8. Break the onigirazu in the quarter when the nori sheet has cooled, then serve in bento.

Spinach and Bacon Mini Quiches

Cooking Time: 23 minutes

Serving Size: 1

Calories: 222.3

Ingredients:

- 4 strips bacon (chopped)
- Dash of pepper
- 6 eggs
- 1 cup cheddar cheese (shredded)
- ¾ cup spinach (chopped)
- 3 tablespoons milk

Method:

1. Set the temperature to 350F (180C) of oven and oil a 24-mini muffin tray.

2. Whisk the milk and eggs together in a large cup.

3. Add the chopped kale, sliced cheddar, seasoning and minced bacon.

4. To blend all the items, give it a fast shake.

5. Uniformly distribute beaten eggs into muffin pan containers.

6. Put for 15-20 minutes in the oven and bake.

7. Enable the mini-quiches to chill in the pan until baked before removing them with a sharp knife or slotted spoon. Put in bento box once cooled.

Tonkatsu Bento

Cooking Time: 20 minutes

Serving Size: 1

Calories: 948

Ingredients:

- Broccoli
- Salad dressing
- Lettuce
- Radish
- Japanese short-grain rice (Cooked)
- Tonkatsu sauce
- Tomatoes
- Tonkatsu (pre-cooked)

Method:

1. Fill the Japanese rice with a quarter of the bento box.

2. Let everything cool, so other cool meals are not warmed up by hot rice.

3. Take the remaining tonkatsu from the refrigerator and cook in a toaster oven for several minutes until it becomes warm.

4. On top of the rice, place tonkatsu and scatter tonkatsu Sauce on top.

5. Wash and dry the lettuce, tomatoes, and radish. If required, cut.

6. Put the broccoli neatly in the bento box.

7. Pour the dressing into a container with the sauce.

8. Before shutting the bento box, cool down entirely.

Ginger Pork Onigirazu Bento

Cooking Time: 15 minutes

Serving Size: 1

Calories: 648

Ingredients:

- Japanese mayonnaise
- Ginger Pork
- 1 sheet nori (seaweed)
- kosher salt
- 1 leaf lettuce
- 1 cup of Japanese rice (cooked)

Method:

1. On a working surface, put a plastic wrap and place a layer of nori seaweed on edge (glossy side down).

2. Scatter the boiled rice equitably in a thin layer and shape at the core of the nori sheet into a square shape.

3. Scatter with some kosher salt.

4. Put the vegetables on top and put some Japanese mayo on top of the rice.

5. Put the ginger meat on top then. Consider how you will cut the onigirazu later when you insert the fillings.

6. You have to arrange fillings, so the products are disclosed in a way when you cut the onigirazu in the quarter so that it looks delicious.

7. Put a nice rectangular shape on the edge of a small piece of steamed rice.

8. If you have an onigirazu mould, before pressing down, wet the lid so that rice does not get locked to it.

9. Put on top of the lid and carefully place.

10. Slowly lift the mould up whereas the lid is pressed down. Please ensure to stack the food items nicely if you are not using a mould.

11. Carry the nori sheet's left side corners and toward the middle. To toss around the rice and fill in the middle, fold softly but closely.

12. Then bring the lower and upper corners to the centre. Proceed to fold around from the pieces gently but tightly.

13. Ensure that the rice is neatly clipped in. In a plastic wrap, cover securely.

14. Put aside for five minutes with the seam side down for nori.

15. Break the onigirazu with a sharp blade after five minutes. Within 24 hours, eat.

Sweet and Sour Chicken Bento

Cooking Time: 20 minutes

Serving Size: 1

Calories: 457

Ingredients:

- Toasted black sesame seeds
- Japanese pickled plum
- Japanese short-grain rice (cooked)
- Japanese potato salad
- Cherry tomatoes
- Chicken
- Ramen egg

Method:

1. Pack third of the bento box with steamed rice and then let it cool.

2. In a deep fryer, reheat the ootaxa's sweet and savoury chicken until warmed.

3. Move them and then let them cool on a small dish.

4. In the meantime, put in the bento box the Ajitsuke Tamago, mashed potatoes, and fresh tomato.

5. Load in the bento box if the sweet and savoury chicken is cool.

6. Entirely cool down to avoid moisture before shutting down the bento box.

Teriyaki Salmon Bento

Cooking Time: 15 minutes

Serving Size: 1

Calories: 540

Ingredients:

- Gyoza
- Raspberries
- Japanese short-grain rice (cooked)

- Broccoli
- Teriyaki Salmon

Method:

1. Fill the Japanese rice to a quarter of the bento box.

2. Let everything cool so that other chilled food is not warmed up by hot rice.

3. Cook the Teriyaki Salmon and Gyoza leftovers in a skillet or cook them in a deep fryer until hot.

4. Wash fruit and dry thoroughly. Placed them neatly together with broccoli in the bento box.

5. Before shutting the bento box, cool down entirely.

Miso Yaki Onigiri

Cooking Time: 30 minutes

Serving Size: 6

Calories: 249

Ingredients:

- kosher salt
- ½ tablespoon neutral-flavoured oil
- 2 tablespoon miso
- 10-12 shiso leaves
- 2 teaspoon toasted white sesame seeds
- 1 teaspoon sugar
- 3 cups Japanese rice (cooked)
- Uncooked rice
- 1 tablespoon mirin

Method:

1. Put two tablespoons of miso, 1 teaspoon of sugar, and 1 teaspoon of mirin in a shallow saucepan and blend well.

2. It may be sweeter or saltier than normal, based on the form of miso.

3. By extracting/inserting sugar, change the taste.

4. To clean the rice balls eventually set the sauces aside.

5. Hold six shiso leaf aside for preparing the rice ball.

6. Roll up the remaining leaves of the shiso and cut into slices in julienne.

7. In a fried rice cup, add shiso leaf and fried white sesame seeds, fluff up the rice using a rice scooper as you blend in shiso leaves and sesame seeds.

8. Make a small pan of water and a dash of kosher salt, around two to three teaspoons.

9. Moist your hands with water, touch the salt with your fingertips and gently rub some of the salt on your hands.

10. Then pick 1/6 of the fried rice section using a rice scooper.

11. Form the rice softly into a tight ball, then squeeze the upper part. It is supposed to look like the thick form of a disk.

12. Brush the parchment paper with oil. Put the balls of rice and begin to cook on medium-high heat.

13. Ensure that some gap among rice balls is preserved so that they do not bind to each other.

14. For around five minutes, steam the base of the rice.

15. Rub the oil on the surface of the rice balls when it is nicely golden and turn to roast the other surface for five minutes or until it is nicely golden.

16. Decrease the temperature to low heat if both surfaces are perfectly brown.

17. On tops of the rice balls, put the sauce. Then turn to bake for just 15 seconds on the miso edge.

18. Then move to the other side of the sauce to clean and cook for 15 seconds.

19. Serve on shiso leaves with each rice ball in the bento box.

Braised Pork Belly Bento

Cooking Time: 15 minutes

Serving Size: 1

Calories: 410

Ingredients:

- Tomatoes
- Furikake (rice seasoning)
- Tamagoyaki
- Broccoli
- Braised Pork Belly
- Japanese short-grain rice (cooked)

Method:

1. Fill the Japanese rice with a quarter of the bento box.

2. Let it chill so that other cool food is not warmed up by hot rice.

3. In a deep fryer, reheat the leftover stewed pulled pork until completely hot.

4. In a silicon cup, pack cooled the braised pulled pork and placed it in a bento box.

5. Placed the Tamagoyaki in the bento box with the vegetables.

6. Wash your vegetables and pat them dry. Place it nicely in a box of bento.

7. Spray on top of the rice with furikake.

8. Before shutting the bento box, cool down entirely.

Egg Salad Sandwich Bento

Cooking Time: 10 minutes

Serving Size: 1

Calories: 582.8

Ingredients:

- freshly ground black pepper
- pinch sugar
- 1 tablespoon Japanese mayonnaise
- kosher salt
- 2 slices bread of your choice
- 1 hard-boiled egg (peeled)

Method:

1. Collect all the ingredients.
2. Take the boiled egg and mash with a fork.
3. Now add three tablespoons of mayonnaise.
4. You may add ½ it is not moist. Mix with salt and pepper.
5. Place a bit of bread with the beaten egg on front and place some piece of bread on top.

6. Break the bread's sides off.

7. Typically, Japanese sandwiches do not have sides.

8. Based on the bento box width, slice the sandwiches into 2-3 sections.

9. In the bento box, load the sandwiches and place some vegetables and fruit in space.

Gyoza Bento

Cooking Time: 20 minutes

Serving Size: 1

Calories: 590

Ingredients:

- Cucumber (pre-cooked)
- Furikake (rice seasoning)
- Japanese short-grain rice (cooked)
- Broccoli
- Tamagoyaki
- Gyoza (pre-cooked)
- Tomatoes
- Lettuce
- Soy sauce

Method:

1. Fill the Japanese rice to half of the bento box. Let it chill, so another cool item is not warmed up by hot rice.

2. Pan Fry the leftover Gyoza or cook till it is hot in a deep fryer.

3. In a saucepot, pack the soy sauce.

4. Wash the lettuce and tomatoes and wipe them dry.

5. Put the broccoli beautifully in the bento box.

6. Pack tamagoyaki cooled Gyoza and cucumber chikuwa.

7. Spray on top of moderately cooled rice with furikake.

8. Before shutting the bento box, cool down entirely.

Bento Bowl with Sesame Tofu

Cooking Time: 30 minutes

Serving Size: 4

Calories: 566.5

Ingredients:

Pickles

- A slice of raw beetroot
- ½ teaspoon turmeric
- 2 piece of ginger
- ¼-½ cup sugar
- 1½ teaspoon fine sea salt
- 1 cup of rice vinegar
- 1 daikon

Tofu

- ¼ cup cornflour
- 3 tablespoon oil for frying
- 200g tofu (pressed)
- 1 teaspoon white sesame seeds
- ½ cup Aquafaba (reduced)

- 2 tablespoon tamari
- 1 cup Panko
- 2 teaspoon black sesame seeds
- 2 teaspoon Sriracha

Remaining Ingredients

- Tamari or soy sauce
- Chilli sauce
- Stir-fried veggies
- Favourite rice (cooked)

Method:

1. Slice the ginger and daikon.

2. Cut the ginger as finely as you can and cut the daikon into slightly bigger pieces.

3. Rub the ginger pieces with half a teaspoon of salt and set aside for thirty minutes. Rinse the salts off after 30 minutes.

4. In a shallow dish, add rice vinegar, ½ bowl of water, sugars and one teaspoon of salt and bring to the boil.

5. If you plan to dye the ginger peach and the daikon orange, prepare two small pots.

6. To dye it pink, apply a strip of beetroot to the ginger and turmeric to the daikon to colour it orange. For the day, set aside.

7. In a small dish, add two tablespoons of tamari and two tablespoons of Sriracha. Mix thoroughly.

8. In the soy-Sriracha mix, cut the stretched tofu block into twelve even parts and position them.

9. By spooning a few of the marinade over the surface of the sliced tofu, make sure that the bits are mixed thoroughly. Leave for fifteen minutes to refrigerate.

10. In the meantime, prepare three shallow pots, that of sesame seeds, the other with Aquafaba, and the third with cornflour combined with breadcrumbs.

11. When using breadcrumbs, smash them a little and get rid of big bits in a pestle and mortar as they would not stick too well to the tofu.

12. Cover each square of tofu with cornflour, then with Aquafaba and finally with breadcrumbs.

13. To obtain an even coverage on all levels, ensure you press each side of the square into the powder and cornflour properly.

14. If you want a finer crust, once you have made the first layer, you can roll the tofu again in the Aquafaba and cornflour. In a griddle, pour 2-3 tablespoons of oil and warm it.

15. Cook the tofu in groups of six once the oil is heated.

16. Shift the temperature down to the minimum so that the parts do not brown too easily. They should be on either side for around two minutes.

17. Place the tofu on a sheet of paper towel to extract excess fat until the first batch is prepared, and begin frying the second batch.

18. Serve the tofu directly from the skillet, with pickles and seasonings on one side on top of basic cooked rice with stir-fried vegetables in the bento box.

No-Cook Greek Pita Bento Box

Cooking Time: 25 minutes

Serving Size: 4

Calories: 308

Ingredients:

- 2 tablespoons feta cheese (crumbled)
- olives (to taste)
- 12 slices deli chicken
- ½ bell pepper (chopped)
- ¼ cup red onion (diced)
- 1 cup tzatziki
- 1 cup cherry tomatoes
- 2 cups cucumber (diced)
- Greek Salad
- 12 mini pitas

Method:

1. Mix all of the Greek salad items.
2. Split between the four lunch boxes for bento.
3. Divide the majority of the ingredients into bento lunch boxes.

Honey Sesame Chicken with Broccoli Bento Box

Cooking Time: 35 minutes

Serving Size: 4

Calories: 377

Ingredients:

Chicken

- 2 garlic cloves (minced)
- 1 tablespoon vegetable oil
- 1 pound chicken thighs

- 1 tablespoon sesame oil
- 1 tablespoon ginger (grated)
- Kosher salt
- 3 tablespoons soy sauce
- 3 tablespoons honey
- ⅓ cup chicken broth
- Freshly ground black pepper

Sides

- 2 tablespoons sesame seeds
- 1 bunch scallions (sliced)
- Freshly ground black pepper
- 1 cauliflower rice
- 1 tablespoon sesame oil
- Kosher salt
- 2 bunches broccoli (trimmed)

Method:

1. Heat the 425°F oven.
2. Use salt and black pepper to spice the chicken.
3. Mix all the chicken stock, soy sauce, sugar, sesame oil, garlic and ginger in a moderate dish.
4. Heat the oil in a big oven-safe saucepan over medium heat.
5. In the pan, add the chicken, skin down flat, and fry until golden brown uniformly, about five minutes. Turn the side of your chicken skin.
6. Load the broth solution into the pan and boil for two minutes over medium-high heat.

7. Move the pan to the preheated oven for 15 to 17 minutes, till the liquid has caramelized and the chicken is thoroughly cooked.

8. Mix the broccoli and sesame oil in a wide bowl; sprinkle with salt. On a baking tray, place a layer.

9. Grill the broccoli till it is soft, ten to fifteen minutes although the chicken finishes frying.

10. Split the cauliflower rice and broccoli into several pots to combine the meal-prep pots.

11. Transfer the chicken, sesame seeds and green onions to the garnish.

12. Present or chill in the fridge instantly for up to 4 days.

No-Cook Taco Salad Bento Box

Cooking Time: 25 minutes

Serving Size: 4

Calories: 222

Ingredients:

- 1/8 teaspoon salt
- 1 teaspoon lime juice
- 1 cup black beans
- 1 jalapeno pepper (chopped)
- pico de gallo
- 4 Roma tomatoes (chopped)
- 2 tablespoons red onion (chopped)
- ½ cup dressing of choice
- tortilla chips
- 3 cups romaine lettuce (chopped)

- ½ cup cheese (shredded)
- 1 cup corn kernels

Method:

1. Divide the components into 4 containers for storage.
2. To continue dressing separately until a week before serving, use a sauce container.
3. Mix the pico de gallo components and apply them to the boxes.
4. Hold it in the refrigerator for up to four days.
5. You will need to bring an extra bowl for the salad to be served.

Sheet Pan Garlic Ginger Chicken and Broccoli Bento

Cooking Time: 15 minutes

Serving Size: 4

Calories: 409

Ingredients:

For the Garlic Ginger Sauce

- ¼ cup white vinegar
- ½ cup of water
- ¼ cup oil
- 2-inch knob ginger (peeled)
- 4 Medjool dates
- ¾ cup soy sauce
- 4 cloves garlic

For the Chicken and Broccoli

- Sesame seeds

- Green onions
- 1 pound chicken breasts
- 1 red pepper
- Sesame oil
- 1 head broccoli

Method:

1. Heat the oven to a temperature of 425 degrees. Mix all of the sauce components until creamy.

2. On a sheet pan, put chicken, vegetables, and red pepper.

3. On the base of the chicken, add about half a cup of sauce and just a few more tablespoons of sauce over the vegetables. Bake for around 10-15 minutes.

4. When frying vegetables and chicken, boil another half a cup or so of sauces over moderately low heat in a small pan once caramelized.

5. Sprinkle the cooked chicken and vegetables over it.

6. Use sesame oil, pumpkin seeds, or scallions to finish. Serve in the bento box.

Slow-Cooker Burrito Bowls Bento

Cooking Time: 7 hours 15 minutes

Serving Size: 4

Calories: 508

Ingredients:

- 1 tablespoon cumin powder
- 1 teaspoon garlic powder

- 1½ pounds pork shoulder
- One 4-ounce can green chilis
- 2 teaspoons coriander powder
- Kosher salt
- Ground black pepper
- Juice of 1 orange
- Juice of 2 limes
- ¼ cup beef broth
- 2 tablespoons olive oil

Sides

- ½ Cup cilantro leaves
- 1 Fresno chilli (sliced)
- ⅓ cup Greek yogurt
- 2 avocados (sliced)
- 1 head romaine (shredded)
- 3 limes
- Ground black pepper
- One can black beans
- ½ teaspoon taco seasoning
- ½ red onion (minced)
- Kosher salt
- 1-pint cherry tomatoes

Method:

1. Dress the meat with pepper and salt.
2. Add the oil in a frying pan over medium heat.

3. Insert the pork and cook until it turns golden brown, 10 minutes on all directions.

4. In the slow cooker, move the pork. Mix beef stock, fruit juice, lemon juice, chilli peppers, cilantro, cumin and garlic powder to taste.

5. Switch the cooker down and cook for about seven hours until the pork is ready. With two forks, cut the pork.

6. Mix Greek yogurt, half lemon juice, and taco spice in a shallow saucepan.

7. Toss together all the tomatoes, spring onion and half lemon juice in a medium bowl; sprinkle with salt.

8. Split the sliced pork between four boxes, filling only a third of each one, to combine.

9. Create a row of tomato combination next to the beef, then a line of black beans, then a line of pieces of avocado, and then a line of Roman lettuce.

10. Garnish with cilantro, chilli pepper and leftover lemons, split into slices.

11. Drizzle on top of the yogurt solution just before eating.

Creamy Kale Caesar Salad Bento

Cooking Time: 15 minutes

Serving Size: 4

Calories: 243

Ingredients:

- ¼ teaspoon salt
- Freshly ground black pepper
- 1 large bunch kale
- 1 tablespoon lemon juice

- 1 garlic clove (minced)
- ¼ cup (grated) Parmesan cheese
- 3 tablespoons olive oil
- ¼ cup sour cream
- ⅓ cup (chopped) walnuts (toasted)

Method:
1. Pull from the kale and cut the wide stems and middle sections and split the leaves into thin strips.
2. Mix it with the toasted walnuts in a large mixing bowl.
3. Stir the sour cream, olive oil, parmesan, lime juice, garlic, salt and black pepper with each other in a shallow saucepan to flavour.
4. Stir the dressing over the combination of kale, coat it and eat this within one day.

Tuna Protein Box

Cooking Time: 20 minutes

Serving Size: 4

Calories: 414

Ingredients:
- 1 cup blueberries
- 8 oz. cheese (cubed)
- 4 whole eggs
- 2-3 ribs celery (chopped)
- 1 cup grapes
- 4 carrots (chopped)

Tuna Salad

- 2 tablespoons celery (chopped)
- Salt and pepper to taste
- 2 tablespoons mayonnaise
- 5 oz. can of tuna (drained)

Method:

1. Cook the hard-boiled eggs and cool them.
2. When they have settled fully, you need to keep them on with the shells or strip them.
3. Mix the food items for the tuna salad and split between jars.
4. Split among jars all other spices.
5. Up to four days, you can store in the refrigerator. Eat once cold.

Honey Lemon Chicken Bowls Bento

Cooking Time: 35 minutes

Serving Size: 6

Calories: 272

Ingredients:

Lemon Honey Chicken Bowls

- 2 pounds of chicken breasts
- 6 cups (cooked) rice
- Kosher salt
- Freshly-cracked black pepper
- 2 tablespoons olive oil (divided)
- 2 cups (small) broccoli florets

- 1 pound fresh asparagus

Honey Lemon Sauce

- pinch of ground ginger
- 2 cloves garlic
- ¼ cup chicken broth
- 1 tablespoon soy sauce
- 1 teaspoon sesame oil
- ¼ cup lemon juice
- 1 tablespoon cornstarch
- ¼ cup honey

Method:

1. In a big sauté griddle or skillet over medium temperature, heat 1 tablespoon of butter or oil.

2. Add the vegetables and asparagus and sprinkle with salt. Sauté for five minutes, until soft, stirring occasionally.

3. To a plate or bowl, move the asparagus and vegetables and transfer the skillet to the temperature.

4. Insert to the skillet, together with the chicken, the residual 1 tablespoon oil. With salt and black pepper, season the meat.

5. Sauté for 5-6 minutes till the meat is cooked through and no longer pink inside, tossing occasionally.

6. Stir in the lemon sauce with the honey till the chicken is uniformly coated, and cook for 1 minute or until the sauce cooks and softens.

7. Withdraw the pan from the heat.

8. Among 6 food glass jars, section the rice, veggies and chicken equitably.

9. Top it with the garnishes you want. Then serve right away, or fill and chill in the fridge for up to four days.

10. In a shallow saucepan or Mason jar, stir all spices together until mixed.

Chicken Patty Bento

Cooking Time: 40 minutes

Serving Size: 2

Calories: 665

Ingredients:

- 2 radishes
- Salad dressing of choice
- 2 cups rice (uncooked)
- Salad
- 2 cups spinach
- Chicken patties
- 1 teaspoon sesame oil
- 1 tablespoon sesame seeds
- 1 teaspoon chilli paste
- 3 tablespoon vegetable oil
- 2 tablespoon hoisin sauce
- 1 tablespoon soy sauce
- 1 stalk green onions
- 1 lb. Ground chicken

Method:

1. Start by cleaning the rice and boiling it on the box according to the instructions.

2. For the salad, wipe the veggies and radishes and let them dry apart.

3. Slice them into small strips while the radishes are clean. Just put aside.

4. Wash the spring onions, then soak it into thin pieces.

5. Mix the ground chicken, roasted spring onions, hoisin seasoning, soy sauce, sesame and spicy seasoning in a mixing bowl and stir well to create the patties.

6. Split it up of meat into eight even bits and form them into patties.

7. Warm the sesame oil and vegetable oil in a frying pan over medium-high heat.

8. Put the patties on and roast each edge for approximately five minutes once the pan gets hot.

9. Place them on a tray once all the patties are cooked thoroughly and leave to cool off moderately.

10. You can start assembling it when you finish cooking all the various portions of a bento box.

11. Squeeze into each tray about 1 bowl of rice and start moving it to one edge.

12. If you do not have a split jar, use bits of spinach to divide the various parts.

13. Besides the rice, place two to three patties.

14. You could even put them on top of the rice to make room for both the salad if you have a broader bag.

15. To complete the remainder of the jar, insert the spinach and the cut radish.

16. In a separate small jar, prepare the salad dressing. Close box of bento and serve.

Tuna-Apple Bento Box

Cooking Time: 25 minutes

Serving Size: 2

Calories: 414

Ingredients:

- Wheat crackers
- Escarole leaves
- 3 tablespoons lemon juice
- Mayonnaise
- Fresh basil leaves (chopped)
- ½ bulb fennel (sliced)
- Jar of tuna in oil
- 1 tablespoon Dijon mustard
- Sugar
- Freshly ground pepper
- 1 apple
- ¼ cup olive oil
- Kosher salt

Method:

1. Mix kosher salt and freshly ground black pepper; mix lime juice, Dijon mustard, a touch of syrup, and additional olive oil.
2. Slice the apple into toothpicks and apply the dressing and flip.

3. Add in the oil, diced fennel and a can of tuna; turn to mix.

4. Pack a bento box or other jar capable of resealing.

5. Mix all the mayonnaise and fresh herbs leaves, coarsely diced; season with salt.

6. Load your bento box in a tiny container.

Kale Cobb Salad Work Lunch

Cooking Time: 15 minutes

Serving Size: 4

Calories: 632

Ingredients:

- ¼ teaspoon salt
- ¼ teaspoon black pepper
- 2 chicken breasts (grilled)
- 1 tablespoon Dijon mustard
- 2 teaspoon olive oil
- ¼ cup mayo
- ½ cup (grated) cheese
- 3 cups kale
- 1 lemon (juiced)
- 2 eggs, hard-boiled
- 1 avocado
- 10 grape tomatoes
- 4 slices bacon (cooked)
- 1 cob corn (grilled)

Method:

1. Chop the pork, cut some of Cobb's corn kernels, cut the tomatoes and grind the cheese.

2. Slice them, and mix them softly with a squeeze of lime or lemon juices for the avocado.

3. In the small bites of your bento case put all these items.

4. Combine the mayo, vinegar, lime juice, and salt and black pepper just to make the topping.

5. Slice the kale into serving sizes pieces and put them in a dish.

6. Sprinkle with a thin pinch of olive oil and salt. Pull and rub the kale till it becomes soft, using your palms.

7. On edge, add the coating and mix until the kale is covered uniformly.

8. Put the kale in your bento boxes with the larger part.

9. Top with chicken breasts diced and a boiled egg cut in half. Serve in the bento box.

Conclusion

Sushi is a famous Japanese food that is now recognized worldwide. Sushi is a popular dish of vinegar rice cooked with several flavours, such as fish, sometimes raw, and veggies, typically with some salt and sugar. The sushi wraps (maki) are one of several types of sushi. Soy sauce and wasabi are the essential seasonings used with sushi. As a side dish, soy sauce is being used, and wasabi is put into nigiri-sushi and can also be combined for eating with soy sauce. At the same time, Bento is a type of lunch box which has compartments to put a different kind of foods. There are many restaurants of sushi all around the world. Sushi has many health benefits as it has Omega3, which decrease heart and skin diseases. It nourishes the brain and helps fasten your memory. It is suitable for women suffering from osteoporosis. Sushi is good to keep your muscles in a good state. Different delicious and easy to make recipes are given in this book consisting of sushi and Bento. The first thing you have to do is to start reading the different cooking styles of bento and sushi in this book and increase your sense of taste for real Japanese food.

Chinese Home Cooking

The Easy Cookbook to Prepare Over 100 Tasty, Traditional Wok and Modern Chinese Recipes at Home

By

Adele Tyler

The trademarks that are used are without any consent, and the publication of the trademark is without permission or backing by the trademark owner. All trademarks and brands within this book are for clarifying purposes only and are owned by the owners themselves, not affiliated with this document.

Table of Contents

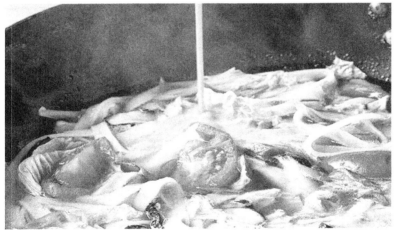

Introduction

Chinese cuisine developed from different areas of China and soon became very popular around the world for its unique cooking style and flavor. There are eight central cuisines in china. Chinese foods are mainly comprised of two components that are grains and meat. Starch and vegetables are essential ingredients of all dishes. The necessary foundation of the most Chinese dishes is garlic, ginger, and sesame. Soy sauce is used in all cuisines for saltiness.

Stir-frying is an essential technique to cook Chinese cuisines. A wok is used to stir-fry vegetables in garlic. Wok dishes are the most common and widespread in America. Chinese cuisine got popular when Chinese immigrants came to America and worked in food shops.

Many traditional Chinese dishes gained popularity in America. Thus, many chefs in the United States made a bit changes in Chinese cooking style, hence Chinese-American dishes emerged.

Chinese cuisine is not only tasty but also healthy and nutritious. Spices used in Chinese cooking are full of nutrients that a human body needs to work the whole day. These are a rich source of carbohydrates, starch, proteins, and fibers. This book "Chinese Home Cooking" will explain Chinese cuisine and its early history. The first chapter will introduce Chinese food and its emergence from the Zhou dynasty to the Ming Dynasty, how it has evolved from time to time, and has become famous in the United States.

The second chapter is a brief discussion about the benefits of the Chinese cuisine. Moreover, it will help you enhance your cooking skills through specific techniques used in Chinese restaurants. This chapter will also tell you the difference between Chinese traditional home cooking and restaurant cooking style. The third chapter is about breakfast and appetizer recipes to make you start your day with delicious and quick recipes. The fourth Chapter is about lunch and snack recipes to regain the energy you have wasted during your work. The fifth chapter includes dinner and dessert recipes to make tasty food for your family meal with some sweet dishes and side dishes.

The last chapter will provide you three different kinds of meals, including traditional wok recipes, famous recipes known worldwide, and, the most importantly, vegetarian recipes. You can choose to make these recipes in your special events or family gatherings.

Finally, a brief conclusion about choosing Chinese cuisine for you and your family are given to help you support your idea of selecting Chinese food.

So, start reading this book and enhance your cooking knowledge and cooking skills with "Chinese Home Cooking".

Chapter 1: Origin and Historical Background of Chinese Food

China is the country with the most prominent citizens and the nation with the highest and most innovative cuisine in the world. The general name for dishes from different regions and ethnicities in China is Chinese cuisine. With excellent infrastructure, rich divisions and institutions, and a distinctive theme, it has a long history. It is the crystallization of the past of thousands of years of Chinese cuisine. A significant aspect of Chinese culture, also known as the Chinese culinary tradition, is Chinese cuisine. Chinese cuisine is one of the triple international cuisines and has a far-reaching influence on the East Asian region. The ingredients are sourced from different areas and cultural dishes.

Chinese Cuisine in the Zhou Dynasty

According to ancient records, China already had a barbecue, fried fish, and other foods more than 5000 years ago.

Food was primarily grains such as peas, buckwheat, corn, and brown rice during the Zhou dynasty in China, although they were not the same as what we have produced in the modern agricultural industry today. In the late Zhou dynasty, people began to get white rice/peeling rice, which was very rare and expensive and affordable for the wealthy class to consume. Similar to other countries, salt was a key factor in cooking and people's everyday life. By then, salt was widely used already. There was a popular cuisine called 'Ba Zheng' in the Zhou Dynasty, which was quite popular for centuries to come.

Chinese Cuisine in the Qin Dynasty

In the Qin dynasty, the sour taste was accepted by the people at a certain time. Bamboo slides recovered from temples, according to historical documents, berries were another hot cooking by then. It was primarily used for extracting fishy unusual from meat or fish inferred by academics. Besides, during the Qin dynasty, cinnamon, spring onions, canola source, and cider were also used in the cooking.

Chinese Cuisine in Han Dynasty

When it came to the Han dynasty, salty taste was preferred. Han was a time when Chinese cuisine took a major move forward. There were many "foreign-made" food and cooking ingredients for people at the period, such as peppers, grapefruit, oranges, hazelnuts, cardamom, pineapple, pomegranate, broccoli, lettuce, thyme, fennel, spinach, garlic, and onion, owing to the opening of the Silk Road in the Han Dynasty, for traders and commercial trade. In the later tang dynasty, this lay a strong cornerstone for the advances of Chinese cuisine. Chinese cuisine quickly evolved during the Han, Wei, northern and Southern Dynasties, and many popular cuisines emerged.

Chinese Cuisine in Tang Dynasty

Chinese cuisine had already grown to a standard of quality by the period of the Tang dynasty. People also had several types of gatherings or cocktail parties to live their time at a certain period.

Chinese Cuisine in the Song Dynasty

The Song Dynasty is among the stars of the history of Chinese cuisine. There were various cold meals, hot meals, soups, and decorative dishes at Bianjing and Linen's menus. The dishes were labeled with North, South, Chuan flavors, and vegetable meals, which indicated that cuisines' institutions started to develop.

Chinese Cuisine in Yuan, Ming, and Qing Dynasty

During the Yuan, Ming, and Qing Dynasty, Chinese cuisine had a huge success. Hundreds of cuisines emerged. During this time, ethnicities believed in Islamism, migrated to all parts of China, and halal certification occupied China's role as a new form of Chinese food. Since the Qing Dynasty was a king ruling under the Manchu people, Manchu style and flavors were introduced to Chinese cuisine. During the Ming Dynasty of this time frame, chilled pepper crops were introduced as an elegant plant in China. It did not take too long until Chinese people learned its high benefit in cooking methods. The spicy flavor soon became popular in Hunan and Sichuan provinces at that period and had since left a massive impact on their cooking style. Chinese cuisine schools were founded. From the late Qing Dynasty and outsiders came to China, Chinese cuisine even added some characteristics of western cuisines. In the world, Chinese cuisine is very popular for its color, scent, flavor, and better style.

1.1 History of Traditional Chinese Dishes

Chinese cooking is commonly seen to represent one of the country's wealthiest and most varied cuisine histories and cultures. It emerged in various areas of China, and it has been spread from Southeast Asia to Western Europe and North America to other regions of the world. In Chinese culture, dinner is usually seen as made up of two specific components: (1) a source of starch or carbohydrate and (2) fruit, seafood, pork, or other things corresponding meals.

Rice is a vital component of much of Chinese food, as it is widely known globally. Wheat-based items like noodles and boiled buns play a large role in comparison to South China, where rice is prevalent. Despite the value of rice in Chinese cuisine, it is always the case that no grain would be provided at all on highly formal events; in such a scenario; rice will be offered only if all other dishes existed, or as a consolation dish at the end of dinner. To relieve one's stomach, soup is usually eaten at the end of dinner. Serving soup at the beginning of a meal is still very common nowadays, owing to Western influences.

Chinese cuisine history dates back to approximately 5000 BC. Chinese people have created their special way of cooking meat over this large period. Their ways of defining ingredients to make ideal combos, their multi-method cooking strategies, and their multidisciplinary flavoring management have all been increasingly improved. There was a very good diet for the ancient Chinese, and from historical records, agriculture in China appears to have begun around 5,000 years ago. Both variations and transitions are marked by Chinese cuisine. Since ancient times, food has been at the heart of social life, and many current-day dishes with their variations of fragrance and flavor can be linked back to ancient Chinese food patterns.

Food and art have often been regarded by the Chinese, emphasizing preparing food and how it is consumed.

Chopsticks are the main dining utensil for real food in Chinese culture, while sauces and other fluids are enjoyed with a large, flat-bottomed (historically stainless) spoon. Due to the recent deforestation deficits in china and other Asian countries, wooden chopsticks are decreasing their supremacy; many Chinese dining facilities are considering switching to a more environmentally friendly eating fork and spoon, such as plastics or bamboo chopsticks. In the past, more luxurious items used included silver and gold. On the other side, in small restaurants, plastic chopsticks crafted of bamboo/wood have all replaced recycled ones.

Vegetables: Soy Bean and Cucumber

There were not many types of veggies in ancient China, but vegetables were an important part of people's diets regardless. They consumed vegetables with their main meal, rice, whenever they were able to afford it. During that time, the main vegetables were cucumber and soybean, and when soybeans had become the main grain in ancient China, soybean production can be dated back to 1000 BC. The word Shu means soybean began appearing on brass artifacts from the early Zhou period. Soybeans were also described in the Analects of Confucius in the 5th century BC.

Wine: Rice and Millet

China is considered to be one of the earliest countries to produce wine in the world. Wine has not only been a beverage since its launch, but has also been provided with moral and cultural importance, representing political and social life and design concepts, and even appearing in modern literature.

People started to drink wine during the Shang dynasty (16th to 12th century) and used it to honor the deities; yellow grain wine is probably the first of this kind.

Since the Han and Tang dynasties, all other types of wine are believed to have been produced. Millet wine was released years later, and it was a major success, much more common than tea.

Sorghum

The "camel of crops" is classified as sorghum since it does not require much moisture and develops in the soil in which other grains do not. Also, the cost of grain and fertilizer for sorghum is smaller than for other crops. Dating back to the Stone Age is the use of sorghum. A significant volume of carbonized sorghum was detected from the feuding State Period in Shijiazhuang. "China is the oldest and greatest Centre for the roots of sorghum," according to the Genomic Resources Center.

Meat: Pork, Chicken, Beef

Pork is China's most widely-eaten meat, including beef, mutton, goat, duck, bird, etc., and other kinds. From 3000 or 4000 BC, the people in china consumed pork, which was indigenous to China, but cattle and sheep were not indigenous, and soon after that they were imported in China from West Asia. Many people used tofu, or bean paste, as a dietary protein source because the beef was too pricey and because Buddhist monks did not consume meat.

Tea

The origin of Chinese tea can be measured to 4,000 years. The Chinese probably drink tea to be an elegant form of art with so many traditions and traditions attached to it. Tea, along with espresso and cocoa, is China's national beverage and is one of the three popular sweet drinks. China firmly considers itself the cradle of tea as China was the first nation to bring its planting strategies, manufacturing, and drinking practices to the rest of the globe.

Tofu

Tofu, or bean paste, is also of Chinese ancestry and is made from soy protein, milk, water, and a coagulating agent. It has been a dietary staple in Chinese and Asian food since prehistoric times, abundant in minerals, low in fat, and full of protein, calcium, and iron. Since it was a great source of vitamins, Chinese doctors considered that meat was an important meal, but only the wealthiest could afford to consume it. A bill was made to remedy this, where any person living in China will get a free cup of tofu each week, which was a combination of sorghum and other stuff like rice to give everyone the same amount of protein as the meat will. It was hard to cook on a massive scale in China at that time, so people might cut their meat into tiny pieces to prepare it. In Western vegetable meals even, tofu has also become a primary ingredient.

Wheat

People began developing and consuming wheat in China about 2500 BC, previously dependent on exports from West Asia, wheat soon became the primary source of carbohydrates. The traditional Chinese people consumed porridge, but they made no bread out of wheat. The key factor for this was that to cook the rolls, the coal they used for the energy was too pricey.

Rice

Rice is indeed a good source of carbohydrates, comparable to millet, grain, and other crops. In China, rice background goes back to the late Stone Age (around 2000 BC). Rice production is believed to have begun in Thailand, but Chinese farmers invented grain rice.

The method of rice cultivation in muddy, natural ponds is called rice paddies.

Rice was used as a commodity in China since prehistoric times, and when we think of Chinese cuisine, rice is most certainly the very first thing you say of. While rice has been growing in China for a long time, that was too cool to grow rice in north china, so wheat and soybeans were farmed anyway. People cooked rice to render it softer by boiling or steaming it, and rice was also used to create a sort of wine called rice wine, which is still drunk in China today.

1.2 Evolution of Chinese Cuisine

The history of Chinese food covers three centuries of recorded history, spanning an unprecedented expansion of food preparations, food preparation methods, and the use of tons of ingredients.

History of Chinese Noodles

One of the important steps of their whole cuisine is Chinese boiling noodles. They can be located within countless recipes in hundreds of combinations, which has sparked the improvements in cooking style over the Chinese country's history and national tastes. The earliest recorded noodles discovered in China date back 4,000 years. They have been found in historical discoveries along China's Yellow River. However, the first definite historical records of noodles are from the period around 25 to 200 AD. when the East Han Dynasty ruled. These early noodles were traditionally made from corn flour, and as years went by, they became even more common. In the Song Dynasty period, noodles could be bought from Chinese restaurants in major cities in China. Noodles are extensively used in China, Korea, the Philippines, Cambodia, Thailand, Vietnam, and others as Chinese presence spread throughout Asia.

One of the three major components is typical noodles made in China: white flour, corn starch, and mung bean flour. They are sliced using one of the five methods until they are baked and used as a component of other foods: Sliced (with the blade from rolled bread sheet), compressed (dough moved by the device into tiny holes), Peel (large bread strips are cut straight into hot water), Pulled (squeezed dough folded to produce thinner layers) and mashed (rolled bread to the shape desired). Without any hesitation, Char kway teow, Cup Noodles Ban mien, Cart noodle, Beef chow fun, Laksa, Lo mien, Zhejiang mien, and Re gan mien are the most common dishes in Chinese food that use noodles.

History of Chinese Sweet Food

Chinese cuisine has become one of the best diverse globally with an amazing array of dairy products invented by Chinese chefs and developed by more than Three thousand years of things change, proximity to trade channels, and local food products availability. China has managed to produce a wide range of desserts, in contrast to thousands of recognizable dishes and a wide range of liquid drinks (both distilled and unsweetened), which can be made on both prepared foods such as fruit and more complex recipes, often requiring preparation that can last many months or years.

Chinese sweets are delicious, but typically with less amount of sugar than Western deserts. They also have a greater proportion of natural fruit products, which can be used as an integral part of the Chinese Ying and Yang custom of consuming "healthy" meals, not only during dinners and with coffee, but also during meal options.

Chinese desserts are typically classified into several major groups, such as pastry products, candy products (including baked wheat goods such as Moon pastries), candies, cookies, rice-based treats, sweet flavorings, desert meringues, caramels, and ice creams.

Traditional Chinese sweets also played a significant role in upholding Chinese lifestyles and the nutrition of many Asian countries, which have established a cultural and economic relationship with China, making Chinese desserts much more popular and broader.

History of Chinese Soups

China has a long tradition of using many kinds of soups in its kitchen, almost always cooked and eaten to provide the meal with nutrition and provide nutrition and be a provider of natural and therapeutic herbs that can improve the vitality and immune function. Although western soups can contain daily products (dairy products or cream) from start to end, Chinese soups are often broth-based, thickened by refined starches of maize or sweet potatoes.

Chinese Pickles History

A big part of the local food is Chinese pickles. In certain variants, fermented veggies or berries are available because Chinese people usually do not consume fresh fruits. They tend to eat them fried, baked, and processed in several other ways, and if food is poorly handled, the processing is better for many reasons, most important. In China, pickled food is processed by soaking and roasting in salt or brine vegetables and fruits instead of fermenting in paste or sauce compounds. Along with a wide range of medicinal herbs and several other components (even beers), it is very popular to dissolve fruits and vegetables in the pickling method. It should be remembered that mainstream medicine and research do not suggest that many marinated foods be used in their everyday diets. Some researchers have found that marinated food can increase cancer risks, and even marinated vegetables have been reported as possible carcinogens by the World Health Organization. Pickled food could also get riddled with different fungi species very quickly, which can increase the carcinogenic potential of certain foods much further.

Chinese Tea History

Tea holds the most significant position in the Chinese cuisine development, having been present in its society for more than 3,000 years and gradually evolving to its present form with each moving century. Chinese heritage holds the evidence of the first tea drinking during the Zhou Dynasty, stretching back to the third century BC, with various reports confirming that they have been used mainly as medicines since the earliest days. The rich noble's use of tea as a treat and community drink helped popularize in the 8th and 9th centuries during the Tang Dynasty. The style of tea preparing, serving, rituals, protocol, procedures, and even cookware used has altered many Chinese imperial dynasties. The Song Dynasty (960-1276, tea pancakes that were ground into flour and combined with warm water) and the Ming Dynasty (1368-1644, Hiqiu tea, song Luo tea, and several others) were the two most important royal dynasties that made popular the dissemination of new varieties of tea throughout Asia. In the late 1700s, new forms of Chinese tea began to grow under the Qing Dynasty.

Chinese tea varieties can be distinguished between trees, regions that have been grown, and processed. Today, beyond any doubt, the most common form of tea is Chinese Green Tea, produced from the "Camellia Sinensis" herb and manufactured with limited oxidation. Not just because of its good taste and body feel, but because of its medicinal qualities that can minimize the risk of cardiovascular disease and certain forms of cancer, improve the metabolism, and this tea was more praised in China.

1.3 Rise of Chinese Food's Popularity in the United States

The first big influx of Asian refugees to America was the "Chinese 49'ers" who settled in the United States a century before the American Revolutionary War and grafted the first Asian food to America. The first multicultural cuisine at the national scale to be heavily commercialized as a form of food specifically cooked and eaten away from family was Chinese food. Food from China started to draw a fast-growing non-Asian customer base of varied different ethnicities in major cities throughout the nation at the turn of the nineteenth century, and Chinese food became the most popular multicultural cuisine throughout the United States by 1980, helped by the resurgence of Chinese immigration to the United States. As one of the two primary sources of jobs for Chinese immigrants and communities for centuries, Chinese cuisine has also been a critical economic lifesaver for Chinese Americans. Hence, its creation is a significant chapter in United States history and a core part of Chinese America's understanding. The numerous and sometimes disparate developments in the United States the Chinese food industry shows that it is currently at an intersection. The future depends on the degree to which Chinese Americans will dramatically shift their impact on the social and political arena and on the willingness of China in its relationship between the two countries to alter the financial system.

The Transplantation of Chinese Food

When the 49'ers entered California through China, Chinese food landed in America in the major gold period, illustrating immigrants' crucial role in implanting regional food to America.

Not because they wished to evangelize their cuisine amongst non-Chinese, but because of its exceptional significance in establishing their culture and identity, Chinese immigrants took their cuisine to the New World.

The implantation of Chinese food coincided with the development of Chinese societies. During this time, food companies represented a critical sector in the ethnic Chinese industry in major California cities, such as San Diego and San Fran. Thirty-three supermarkets, along with seven hotels and five food stores, accounted for almost half of all firms in the developing Chinese settlement of San Francisco in 1857, outstripping all other forms of enterprises. While in the 1870s, laundry stores in San Diego and San Francisco soon outnumbered Chinese food companies, the former were dispersed in numerous parts of their respective localities. By contrast, within Chinatown, the latter was the central component of exchange and established its significance.

Chinese restaurants selling foods became another significant draw for Chinese immigrants in Chinatown and exposed the fundamental importance of food to the Chinese culture. Indeed, the arrival of Chinese restaurants has often marked the start of a society. For instance, in 1849, in San Francisco, four restaurants launched an emerging culture. In the developing Chinese communities in other towns, such as Marysville, restaurants were also present. It was a major Chinese village site, also known as the larger town (san bu) among the Chinese. There were already three restaurants and two Chinese shops in 1853. At inexpensive rates, Chinese restaurants deliver historically recognized cuisine. In the late 1870s, migrants like Ah Quin could buy a meal for as little as 10 cents in San Fran's Chinatown. However, Chinese dining establishments provided a culturally significant room to relax and socialize. The Chicago Post described a respectable Chinese restaurant in the center as "the resort and gathering room of East Asiatic".

The Birth of "Chinese-American Cuisine"

At the beginning of the 20th century, as Chinese restaurants penetrated to non-Chinese neighborhoods, the third stage in Chinese food development and its popularity in America started to establish an omnipotent presence across the country. As a paper published in 1903, "there is scarcely an American city that did not have its Chinese restaurants to which people of all classes want to go." The proliferation of Chinese restaurants beyond Chinatown during this time created a special Chinese cuisine for American customers. The distribution of Chinese food gained from two important interactions that many Chinese Americans had in the service industry: first, their role as household work, which gave them great knowledge of serving food to a non-Chinese customer base; second, their role as laundrymen, from which they knew how to enabled service in non-Chinese neighborhoods.

Not middle-class visitors and affluent enthusiasts, but white people on the fringes of society, such as hippies, African Americans, and refugees like Jews from Eastern Europe, were the customers who helped make Chinese food into the first non-Anglo cuisine to gain national popularity in popular consumption. Unlike the middle-class visitors who, out of interest, dined in Chinatown cafes, these more oppressed Americans became the most loyal customer base, regularly visiting these restaurants inside and outside Chinatown. The latter two parties sponsored Chinese dining institutions in various East Coast cities. "The New York Tribune reported in 1901, describing the importance of Chinese food amongst the less fortunate, "So many who, though having a limited share of the products of this country, still impact 'sportiness' visit the restaurant for its cheapness and rise to enjoy the strongly flavorful dishes. Chinese food gained little intellectual recognition until recently, because of its historical importance and pervasive appearance.

Chapter 2: Cooking Methods and Health Benefits of Chinese Food

Chinese food usually includes those vegetables and spices that are very nutritious and good for health. Although many different and unique techniques to prepare Chinese cuisine at home and restaurants are there. The ingredients used in the Chinese food are rich in carbohydrates, fiber, proteins, and calcium. This chapter will provide you information about different restaurants' techniques to prepare food and the health benefits of the ingredients they use.

2.1 Preparing Chinese Food at Home vs. Eating at Restaurants

The food that is served at home is very close to that served in China's restaurants.

Restaurant food appears to be cooked more intricately than one would usually do at home.

Restaurants often tend to be more creative when making variants on a cooking method, whereas organic cuisine is more conventional and sticks to the standard recipe rigidly. This is only a consequence, though, of one person being a professionally skilled cook, and the other being a distracted wife/husband. China is a large country, and the cuisine has a great deal of variation from region to region.

In comparison, Chinese meals served in restaurants appear to be less nutritious than real Chinese foods available at home. Chefs can do less for the ingredients that their consumers eat, whether it be high sugar or unhealthy fat, which can be seen at any restaurant. Many restaurants buy inexpensive goods to make a full profit while Chinese foods eaten at home are made from the finest and freshest products. Restaurants will usually use an assortment of liquids and herbs to make these dishes taste healthier. While these restaurant dishes may be extremely tasty, they are not as flavorful and delicious as home-cooked meals because they are normally miss-sauced, too much-salted, or sometimes over-rich.

The Chinese food we see in local New York restaurants is somewhat different from the typical Chinese food in Chinese households. The products used are the key contrast between conventional and American Chinese foods. Many American Chinese restaurants replace conventional ingredients for those available in the surrounding areas to cater to the community's citizens. American Chinese diets focus on meats instead of including vegetables such as rice, pasta, and sorghum, including steamed veggies as side dishes.

Thus, restaurants have a huge amount of content to pick from when writing their meals.

On the table, there are sometimes dishes that people don't know how to prepare or have never consumed before only because they are the dishes that are lifted from another part of China.

As many western restaurants modify Chinese and Indian cuisine to fit a western pallet, Chinese restaurants adjust dishes from other regions to meet the local preferences. Thus, if in a style bar, the food you see in the restaurant may be nothing like the typical home-cooked recipe as the chef must have modified it.

One meal that is used in nearly every restaurant is pork over grain. Much as Americans want it, the dish's main emphasis is the pork, using rice to bring variation to the meal. While American Chinese products include corn, they sometimes replace more Western vegetables such as carrot, broccoli, cabbage, tomatoes, and dairy products for the other main vegetables used. The process used in cooking and serving the food is another extremely significant contrast between Chinese domestic cooking and cafeteria cooking. Considering the vast quantities of food that restaurants have to prepare during a normal working day, many restaurants start cooking food the day before delivering it.

Much as restaurant-style and Chinese house style cooking cuisine vary in the products used and in the preparing processes, they also vary in the cooking types overall. Chinese cuisine foods, ranging from simmering to frying, can be cooked in any manner that the person likes. However, most dishes are cooked by frying techniques in Chinese restaurants, using either a wok, a round-bottomed frying container used for stir-frying, or a cooking pot. Even traditional Chinese foods discovered at home commonly use other ways, such as simmering, to cook rice. Usually, Chinese domestic style cooking is much healthy but lacks the taste that can be seen in cooking in the restaurant-style.

2.2 Health Benefits of Chinese Food

Chinese food is very famous, and it contains all the nutrition that a sound metabolism and body require to remain healthy. While Chinese people consume, on average, thirty percent more calories than Americans, and they have the same behavior patterns, they do not have obesity issues. This is because fructose and vitamin free food are avoided in Chinese cuisine.

Vegetables are "add-ons" to other recipes in the West, but vegetables are key in Chinese cuisine. Chinese assume the significant proportion of vegetables can be properly combined with a minor portion of livestock. Meat is important since excess calories are incorporated. Sugar, processed sugars, and high fat ingredients are quite less in Chinese foods, allowing our bodies to know quickly when they are full. This encourages people who consume Chinese food to survive more on sufficient amounts of food and not overfill their bodies with excessive calories. On the other side, the Western diet tricks our bodies into knowing their boundaries even longer than is ideal.

Chinese cuisine also supplements the food consumption by relying much on liquid foods. Western food is mostly dry, making it necessary for customers to drink water during the day. With daily consumption of Chinese food, there is no need for that, and desire would be better managed. You may know that Chinese food is good, but you do not know that it is one of the healthiest foods you can consume, either.

Healthy Carbohydrates

Carbohydrates give the organism the energy it needs to get through the day. They are converted to glycogen by the liver, a readily available resource in the muscles and liver.

Other types of energy resources, including fat, are unreliable. Good carbohydrates, including noodles and rice, are also used in Chinese meals, helping you remain energized without eating too many calories.

Nutritional Balance

It's essential to add carbohydrates, proteins, as well as other nutrients into your meal. Carbs supply the fuel required, while proteins help maintain and build muscle strength. That's why the ideal choice is Chinese food. Vegetables, noodles, or rice are often used in recipes, and any beef, fish, or other protein gives you a nutritious balance. It can be hard to find a meal that combines all these diverse nutritious elements into one dish with other cuisines.

Fiber

Fiber is another vital element, helping the body's digestive process. However, many individuals don't get plenty, so they don't like eating the soft vegetables that supply it. However, Chinese cuisine is remarkable for serving many well-seasoned and fried high-fiber dishes, giving them a more intense flavor.

Nutrition in Spices

Ginger- Ginger has a long history of use in traditional Chinese medicine; it has long been used to relieve vomiting and stimulate the appetite. Newer research has found that ginger can ease morning sickness and provoke pain that comes with osteoarthritis.

Garlic- Pungent garlic was used in traditional medicine to relieve respiratory problems. It has a range of proven health effects, including decreasing cholesterol and the risk of osteoporosis and some cancers, plus these have antibacterial activity.

Sesame Seeds- Sesame seeds are exploding with nutrients, including copper, iron, and calcium, and a heavy amount of fiber, although they are tiny.

Shiitake Mushrooms- Mushrooms add a pleasant aroma and taste to foods and make a perfect substitute for any or all of the meats in some sauces, allowing you to cut calories and maintain taste. A decent source of energy-producing Vitamin B and magnesium and immune-supporting manganese is shiitake mushrooms.

Tofu- Tofu is a perfect source to get a reasonable amount of protein from the vegetable resources. It is also an outstanding source of bone-building calcium and magnesium.

Bok Choy- This part of the cabbage family is rich in immune system-boosting vitamins A and C.

2.3 Specific Cooking Techniques Used in Chinese Restaurants

In China, there have been hundreds of ways of cooking. However, deep-frying, stir-frying, braising, shallow-frying, heating, boiling, and reheating are the most common techniques.

Stir-Frying

The most widely used process is stir-frying. This process cooks the manufactured ingredients for a brief amount of time at high temperatures. As the source of heating, edible oil is being used. Usually, a wok will be used at high temperatures, spices, and seasonings to apply edible oil. Owing to the brief amount of time involved with the process, foods mostly retain their nutrient benefit. Usually, stir-fried meat is moist and crispy, and vegetables are normally soft and crispy.

Deep Frying

Deep-frying requires much more vegetable oil than stir-frying (the component should be entirely immersed in the fat), providing buttery-textured food. The traditional way of making deep-frying dishes is to break the components into medium-sized parts or pieces, soak them in seasoned spices for a while, cover with corn flour and finally fry in warm cooking oil over medium-high heat. The coating thickness will decide the degree of crunchiness and gentleness on the inside and outside of the products used.

Shallow Frying

Shallow-frying is a preparation method requiring fewer oil products than used in deep-frying and less temperature than stir-frying. Shallow-fried foods are typically very delicate inside, becoming golden or mildly burnt externally. The products for shallow-frying are typically split into strips or flat pieces and brushed with herbs and spices. After being processed, the ingredients are also partially brushed with corn flour to make the external skin crispy. When frying, the products should be shallow-fried on one side first and then switched to the other.

Braising

To prepare large-sized foods crumble-in-your-mouth, braising is to add ingredients and flavorings in a wok or a frying pan simultaneously, add in some water, heat it, and then simmer it for an hour more than. The components are usually formed into pieces or stones. To fry dishes by braising, the seasoning mixes, especially the animal products, should be rid of the strange smell in boiling water and washed in clean water first. The sauce is thickened either with corn flour or reduced by simmering eventually.

Steaming

A special form of cooking developed in China is steaming. It is commonly used for steaming tortillas and wontons in northern China, where people survive on wheaten rice. The method involves putting the materials in a steamer basket, which is put over the liquid in a steamer jar. Steamed food provides more nutrients than that which is dissolved into the water for less protein. Quite little edible oil and fewer seasonings are used, so the food's natural taste is preserved and improved.

Roasting

Roasting is to prepare the food over the open fire of coal or in a microwave. Although seasonings are rubbed in from outside, the odor of the food is eliminated. The roast food's surface still gets denser and golden brown, but it preserves and improves flavors. Many products can be fried, like all meat types, just like most root and bulb veggies. To roast poultry, the products must be prepared, processed, and braised with edible oil to avoid moisture in the products during the roasting process.

Chapter 3: Chinese Appetizers and Breakfast Recipes

3.1 Delicious Chinese Appetizer Recipes

Chef John's Shrimp Toast

Cooking Time: 24 minutes

Serving Size: 4

Calories: 212.3

Ingredients:

- 1 tablespoon soy sauce
- 1 egg white
- ½ teaspoon white sugar
- ½ teaspoon paprika
- ½ pound raw shrimp
- ½ cup finely sliced green onions

- 3 garlic cloves
- Salt to taste
- 4 slices white bread
- 1 teaspoon sesame seeds
- 1 tablespoon ginger root
- 1 anchovy filet
- 1 teaspoon sesame oil
- ¼ cup cilantro leaves
- 1 teaspoon Asian fish sauce
- 1 pinch cayenne pepper
- 1 cup of vegetable oil

Method:

1. Blend all ingredients in a food processor and blend until the mixture becomes smooth.
2. Lightly toast slices of bread and paste shrimp mixture over toasts.
3. Cut edges and slice into halves.
4. Add vegetable oil in the skillet and fry until golden brown.
5. Serve hot with green onion.

Pork Dumplings

Cooking Time: 35 minutes

Serving Size: 100 dumplings

Calories: 751.5

Ingredients:

- 5 cups Chinese cabbage

- 100 wonton wrappers
- 1 ¾ pounds pork
- 1 tablespoon fresh ginger root
- 3 tablespoons sesame oil
- 4 cloves garlic
- 2 tablespoons green onion
- 4 tablespoons soy sauce
- 1 egg

Method:

1. In a bowl, combine the soy sauce, pork, sesame oil, green onion, ginger, garlic, egg, and cabbage.
2. Add 1 teaspoon cabbage mixture into each wonton wrapper and form a triangle shape.
3. Steam dumplings for 20 to 25 minutes and serve hot.

Chinese Chicken Wings

Cooking Time: 65 minutes

Serving Size: 12

Calories: 256.1

Ingredients:

- 2 tablespoons garlic powder
- 5 pounds of chicken wings
- 2 cups soy sauce
- 2 cups brown sugar

Method:

1. Mix all ingredients except chicken wings.
2. Heat ingredients until brown sugar melts completely.

3. Pour mixture over chicken wings and wrap the bowl with plastic cover.

4. Marinate chicken for 8 hours in the refrigerator.

5. Heat oven on 365°F.

6. Cover chicken with aluminum foil and bake for 45 minutes in the oven.

7. Remove foil and bake for 15 minutes more.

8. Serve hot with sauce.

Perfect Pot Stickers

Cooking Time: 30 minutes

Serving Size: 6

Calories: 438.5

Ingredients:

- ½ cup green onions
- 1 pinch cayenne pepper
- 1 ½ cups green cabbage
- 3 tablespoons fresh ginger
- 2 tablespoons soy sauce
- 1-pound pork
- 4 cloves garlic
- 1 teaspoon sesame oil

Dipping Sauce:

- ¼ cup of rice vinegar
- ¼ cup of soy sauce

Dough Ingredients:

- ¾ teaspoon kosher salt

- 2 ½ cups all-purpose flour
- 1 cup hot water

Frying:

- 8 tablespoons water for steaming
- 6 tablespoons vegetable oil

Method:

1. Mix green onion, cabbage, pepper, garlic, ginger soy sauce, sesame oil, and pork in a bowl and mix with a fork.
2. Cover with plastic and chill for an hour in the refrigerator.
3. Mix dough ingredients and make the dough.
4. Knead dough until it becomes soft and smooth.
5. Wrap the dough and let it rest for 30 minutes.
6. Cut dough into small pieces and make sticker wrappers.
7. Fill stickers with pork mixture and fold.
8. Mix dipping sauce ingredients to make the dipping sauce.
9. Heat a skillet and put pot stickers in hot oil until golden brown.
10. Drizzle water and steam for 7 minutes or until crispy.
11. Serve with dipping sauce.

Chinese Egg Rolls

Cooking Time: 70 minutes

Serving Size: 20

Calories: 169

Ingredients:

- 8-ounce bamboo shoots
- 1 cup wood ear mushroom
- 4 teaspoons vegetable oil
- 3 large eggs
- 1 teaspoon sugar
- 14-ounce egg roll wrappers
- 1 egg white
- 1-pound roasted pork
- 2 green onions
- 2 ½ teaspoons soy sauce
- 4 cups oil for frying
- 1 medium head cabbage
- ½ carrot
- 1 teaspoon salt

Method:

1. Heat the skillet and add 1 tablespoon oil.
2. Add beaten egg in oil and cook for 2 minutes on low heat.
3. Change side and cook for another 1 minute.
4. Set aside and let it cool and slice into thin strips.
5. Add vegetable oil in skillet and heat remaining ingredients until vegetables are fully cooked.
6. Add sliced egg in vegetables and refrigerate for 1 hour.
7. Take a plastic wrapper and put vegetable mixture.
8. Roll plastic sheet until top corners are sealed.

9. Cover with plastic to avoid drying.

Chinese cabbage Pork Dumplings

Cooking Time: 95 minutes

Serving Size: 10

Calories: 120

Ingredients:

- 1 teaspoon sugar
- 1 teaspoon salt
- 2 ½ cups all-purpose flour
- 1 tablespoon scallions
- ¼ teaspoon salt
- ¾ cup of water
- ½ pound cabbage
- 1 teaspoon rice cooking wine
- 1 tablespoon ginger
- 1-pound pork sirloin

Method:

1. Mix flour and salt.
2. Add water and make an elastic, smooth dough.
3. Rest it for 10 minutes.
4. Divide the dough into small 50 pieces and roll into a thin circle piece.
5. Mix other ingredients and process slowly until well combined.
6. Add the mixture on pieces and make dumplings.
7. Steam for 6 to 7 minutes until cooked.

Chinese-Style Chicken and Mushrooms

Cooking Time: 40 minutes

Serving Size: 4

Calories: 170

Ingredients:

- ½ teaspoon sugar
- 1 garlic clove
- 100 grams of mushrooms
- ½ cup of water
- soy sauce
- olive oil
- 400 grams of chicken
- 3 teaspoons cornstarch
- salt
- black pepper
- 2 teaspoons fresh ginger

Method:

1. Cook mushrooms on low heat in a skillet with olive oil.
2. Cut chicken into pieces and add other ingredients over it.
3. Mix and marinate for 15 minutes.
4. Cook chicken pieces in skillet and add cooked mushrooms.
5. Heat until well cooked.
6. Serve with sauce.

Hand-Pulled Chinese Noodles

Cooking Time: 90 minutes

Serving Size: 4

Calories: 560

Ingredients:

- 2 teaspoons chili oil
- ¼ cup of soy sauce
- black sesame seeds
- 1 Thai Chile
- 3 ½ cups all-purpose flour
- ½ teaspoon kosher salt
- 1 green onion
- 4 teaspoons toasted sesame oil

Method:

1. Mix flour and salt.
2. Add water and make the dough.
3. Rest the dough for 30 minutes and cut into small pieces.
4. Pull these pieces into thin sticks.
5. Boil this for 10 minutes and rest aside.
6. Heat the skillet and add other ingredients to cook.
7. Add hand-pulled noodles and cook for more 2 minutes.
8. Serve with sauces.

Crispy Sesame Tofu and Broccoli

Cooking Time: 55 minutes

Serving Size: 4

Calories: 370

Ingredients:

- ½ teaspoon salt
- ¼ teaspoon pepper
- 2 scallions
- ¾ pound broccoli florets
- 2 teaspoons sesame seeds
- 1 garlic clove
- 3 tablespoons light brown sugar
- 4 teaspoons rice vinegar
- ½ inch fresh ginger
- 1-pound extra-firm tofu
- 1/3 cup water
- 2 teaspoons cornstarch
- 1/3 cup tamari
- 1 tablespoon toasted sesame oil
- 1 tablespoon neutral oil

Method:

1. Take tofu and rinse with water.
2. Add broccoli in a pan and heat with little water until broccoli becomes green and crispy.
3. Make tamari sauce with tamari, garlic, ginger, and seasoning.
4. Mix other ingredients and cook on low heat.
5. Cut tofu into small pieces and put mixture with a spoon.

6. Heat tofu on low heat until crispy.
7. Heat sauce until bubble comes out.
8. Add broccoli and tofu into the bubbling sauce.
9. Mix for 2 minutes and serve with scallions on top.

Cream Cheese Wontons

Cooking Time: 30 minutes

Serving Size: 6

Calories: 228

Ingredients:

- 8 ounces cream cheese
- ½ teaspoon sugar
- 24 wonton wrappers
- 1 egg beaten
- oil for frying
- 2 teaspoons minced chives
- ½ teaspoon onion powder

Method:

1. Combine and mix sugar, cream cheese, and onion powder.
2. Place a wonton wrapper and put a teaspoon on cream cheese over it.
3. Brush edges with egg and wraps into package shape.
4. Heat pan on 350°F with 4 tablespoon oil.
5. Fry wontons for 6 to 7 minutes or until golden brown.
6. Soak into a paper towel and set aside.
7. Fry all wonton wraps and serve with tamari sauce.

Lumpia Shanghai

Cooking Time: 25 minutes

Serving Size: 6

Calories: 230

Ingredients:

- 3 cups cooking oil
- 50 pieces lumpia wrappers

Filling Ingredients:

- ½ teaspoon black pepper
- ½ cup parsley
- 1 ½ lb. ground pork
- 1 tablespoon sesame oil
- 2 eggs
- 2 pieces onion
- 1 ½ teaspoons salt
- 2 pieces of carrots
- 1 ½ teaspoon garlic powder

Method:

1. Mix all filling ingredients in a bowl and stir.
2. Take lumpia wrap and put fillings on it.
3. Beat an egg and brush it to edges.
4. Roll wrappers and set aside.
5. Heat the skillet with oil and put wrappers into the hot oil.
6. Cook until lumpia floats in oil.
7. Soak extra oil and serve with sauce.

3.2 Chinese Breakfast Recipes

Here are some breakfast recipes to start your day with delicious and easy Chinese dishes to save your energy for the whole day.

Chinese Pork Salad

Cooking Time: 10 minutes

Serving Size: 6

Calories: 124

Ingredients:

- ½ cup stir-fry sauce
- ½ red onion
- 3 ounces chow Mein noodles
- 20 ounces pea pods
- 8 ounces mandarin oranges
- 1-pound pork strips (stir-fry)

Method:

1. Marinate pork strips in the sauce for 25 minutes.
2. Stir-fry pork in a large skillet for 6 to 7 minutes.
3. Mix remaining ingredients in a bowl.
4. Mix pork sauce and mixture.
5. Stir and serve.

Chinese-Style Spareribs

Cooking Time: 2 hours

Serving Size: 6

Calories: 77

Ingredients:

- 3 tablespoons dry sherry
- 2 cloves garlic
- 6 pounds pork spareribs
- 2 tablespoons honey
- 2 tablespoons soy sauce
- ¼ cup hoisin sauce
- ¼ cup of water

Method:

1. Take spareribs and cut them into pieces.
2. Mix all ingredients in a bowl.
3. Take a large sealing bag and put ribs into it.
4. Take ¼ cup of mixture and rest aside.
5. Add the remaining mixture in the bag and mix well with ribs.
6. Marinate mixture in the refrigerator for 1 hour.
7. Heat oven at 350°F and take a baking pan.
8. Put ribs in pan and wrap with baking sheet to bake for 90 minutes.
9. Remove the sheet and put the remaining ¼ cup of mixture on the ribs with a brush.
10. Bake for another 30 minutes.
11. Serve hot with sauce.

Crunchy Chinese Pork Salad

Cooking Time: 20 minutes

Serving Size: 4

Calories: 141

Ingredients:

- 3 ounces chow Mein noodles
- 6 cups iceberg lettuce
- 4 slices bacon
- ½ cup green onions
- 3 tablespoons soy sauce
- 8 ounces water chestnuts
- ¾ pound roasted pork loin
- 1 tablespoon ketchup
- 2 tablespoons honey
- 1 teaspoon mustard

Method:

1. Cook bacon until crisp and set it aside.
2. Take a small bowl and stir ketchup, mustard, and soy sauce together.
3. Take a large bowl and mix pork, bacon, lettuce, green onions, and chestnut together.
4. Add noodles in dressing and salad.
5. Mix well and serve.

Chinese Tomato and Egg Sauté

Cooking Time: 30 minutes

Serving Size: 2

Calories: 810

Ingredients:

- 3 pinches shredded coconut
- black pepper
- 1 tablespoon ketchup
- 1 teaspoon sugar
- 1 cup white rice
- ½ teaspoon sesame oil
- 1 teaspoon cornstarch
- 2 scallions
- 1 heirloom tomato
- 1 tablespoon rice wine
- 2 cups of water
- 4 large eggs
- 1 pinch salt

Method:

1. Chop the scallion and slice tomatoes into very little pieces.
2. Put eggs into a bowl and add seasonings.
3. Add rice wine and beat eggs.
4. Heat wok and add 2 tablespoon oil.
5. Add eggs and scramble. Set aside
6. Heat wok and add 1 tablespoon oil.
7. Add tomatoes and scallions.
8. Stir fry and add seasonings.
9. Add 1 cup of water and cooked eggs.

10. Mix and cover for 2-3 minutes until tomatoes make the paste.

11. Heat until sauce thickens as your requirement.

Chinese Meat Filled Buns (Baozi)

Cooking Time: 1 hour 45 minutes

Serving Size: 16

Calories: 105

Ingredients:

- 3 tablespoons sugar
- 1 teaspoon salt
- 50 milliliters cold water
- 300 grams pork (or chicken)
- 1 teaspoon fresh ginger
- 3 cloves garlic
- 2 spring onion
- 1 tablespoon rice wine
- 1 teaspoon sugar
- 3 shiitake mushrooms
- 2 tablespoons soy sauce
- 1 tablespoon oyster sauce
- 400 grams flour
- 1 ½ teaspoons baking powder
- ½ teaspoon sesame oil
- 3 tablespoons pork lard
- 190 milliliters warm water

- 2 teaspoons yeast

Method:

1. Mix flour, baking powder, yeast, sugar, and salt.

2. Add melted lard and warm water to make the dough.

3. Rest it for 30 minutes and knead until smooth.

4. Take other ingredients and mix them in a processor.

5. Take the dough and cut it into small pieces.

6. Prepare pieces into a circle and put fillings.

7. Roll again in a bun shape and set aside for 30 minutes.

8. Steam buns on a greaseproof paper so that they do not stick with sides of the steamer.

9. Steam for 15 to 20 minutes until it looks shiny and feels like buns.

10. Serve with sauce and lettuce.

Shao Bing - Chinese Breakfast Flatbread

Cooking Time: 65 minutes

Serving Size: 4

Calories: 740

Ingredients:

- 2 teaspoons Sichuan peppercorn
- 1 teaspoon spices
- 1 teaspoon chicken
- ¼ teaspoon salt
- 300 grams plain flour
- 1 tablespoon Chinese cooking wine
- ½ teaspoon salt

- 3 tablespoons vegetable oil
- ¼ cup oil
- 1 tablespoon soy sauce
- 250 grams ground beef
- ¼ cup spring onion
- 2 teaspoons ground ginger
- ¼ cup chopped onion
- 2 teaspoons sesame oil
- ¼ cup chopped coriander
- 2 tablespoons spring onion
- 1 ½ tablespoons flour
- 2 teaspoons white pepper
- sesame seeds

Method:

1. Making Dough- mix flour, salt and sugar in a bowl and mix until lumpy. Add yeast, water, and oil. Knead the dough and cover with plastic wrap. Set aside for 30 minutes.

2. Making Oil Paste- take a small pan and heat oil. Add cake flour and mix until smooth. Continue cooking until aromatic. Let it cool.

3. Heat oven at 425°F.

4. Forming Bread- take dough and roll dough. Add oil paste with spatula and roll dough again. Cut into pieces of bread and add sesame seeds on each bread.

5. Bake breads for 12 to 15 minutes until golden brown.

6. Cut the sides and serve with sauce.

Yang Chow Fried Rice

Cooking Time: 25 minutes

Serving Size: 6

Calories: 120

Ingredients:

- 2 large eggs
- 4 cups day-old rice
- 1 teaspoon toasted sesame oil
- ½ teaspoon kosher salt
- ½ teaspoon chicken bouillon
- ½ pound Chinese BBQ pork
- 3 scallions
- ½ teaspoon white pepper
- 3 tablespoons vegetable oil
- ¼ pound shrimp
- 1 tablespoon soy sauce
- 2 tablespoons oyster sauce

Method:

1. Fry shrimps in 1 tablespoon cooking oil. Set aside.
2. Cook chicken bouillon and scallions until softened.
3. Put rice in a wok and make a hole in the center.
4. Add beaten egg and mix with the rice properly.
5. Add other ingredients and chicken mixture in a pan and stir fry to make a paste.
6. Add paste on top of the rice. Serve hot.

Soya Sauce Mushroom Chicken with Braised Eggs

Cooking Time: 105 minutes

Serving Size: 1

Calories: 118

Ingredients:

- 4 cloves garlic
- 1 teaspoon sesame oil
- 4 eggs
- 3 pieces of chicken thighs
- 150 milliliters chicken broth
- 3 pieces of rock sugar
- 1 tablespoon corn flour
- 3 slices ginger
- 1 tablespoon Chinese cooking wine
- potato
- 6 button mushrooms
- 2-star anise
- 3 tablespoons light soy sauce
- 2 tablespoons dark soy sauce
- 1 dash pepper
- 1 cinnamon stick

Method:

1. Rinse chicken and dry with a towel.
2. Clean mushrooms and marinate chicken for 30 minutes.
3. Soak mushrooms for an hour.

4. Heat oil and add ginger, garlic, anise, cinnamon sticks.

5. Add chicken and stir fry for 5 minutes.

6. Add mushrooms and cook with the chicken for 10 minutes.

7. Add all other veggies and stir.

8. Cook on low heat for more than 20 minutes and add other ingredients.

9. Add corn flour to give thickness to the sauce and serve hot.

Chicken Mustard Green Congee – Chinese Breakfast Rice Porridge

Cooking Time: 55 minutes

Serving Size: 6

Calories: 190

Ingredients:

- ¼ cup mustard greens
- 1 tablespoon sesame oil
- 2 garlic cloves
- ¼ cup chives
- 12 ounces chicken tenderloin
- 1 ginger
- ¾ cup sweet rice
- ½ teaspoon dark soy sauce

Method:

1. Boil ginger, garlic on low heat in a pot, and add chicken.
2. Cook for 20 minutes until chicken cooked properly.
3. Shred chicken and discard ginger garlic.
4. Add rice in chicken broth water and cook for 25 minutes.
5. Add other ingredients and cook for more 5 minutes.
6. Rest aside for 10 minutes and serve.

Loaded Breakfast Baked Potatoes

Cooking Time: 80 minutes

Serving Size: 4

Calories: 470

Ingredients:

- 4 russet potatoes
- teaspoons salt
- teaspoons black pepper
- 2 scallions
- 1 tablespoon butter
- 4 large eggs
- 4 strips bacon
- 2 ounces cheddar cheese
- ½ teaspoon salt
- ¼ teaspoon black pepper
- sour cream
- hot sauce

Method:

1. Heat the oven at 400°F and take an aluminum foil.

2. Pierce potatoes with fork and place on aluminum foil sheet.

3. Bake potatoes for 60 to 70 minutes in the oven.

4. Take the potato and cut lengthwise with a knife to add fillings.

5. Heat the skillet and add other ingredients.

6. Stir until cooked.

7. Add mixture into potatoes and bake again for 10 minutes.

8. Serve immediately.

Baked Hash Brown Cups with Eggs

Cooking Time: 27 minutes

Serving Size: 4

Calories: 420

Ingredients:

- ½ cup shredded cheddar cheese
- chives
- ¼ teaspoon black pepper
- canola oil cooking spray
- 8 large eggs
- canola oil cooking spray
- 1 bag hash brown potatoes
- black pepper
- 4 strips bacon

- ½ teaspoon garlic powder
- salt

Method:

1. Heat oven at 400°F.
2. Place shredded potatoes in a bowl and mix with seasonings.
3. Press potatoes until water leaves.
4. Bake potatoes in muffin cups for 20 to 25 minutes.
5. Heat skillet and add beaten eggs.
6. Stir with a rubber spatula. Do not overcook eggs.
7. Add eggs and seasoning on potato and bake again for 3 to 7 minutes until fully melted.
8. Serve with sauce.

Steamed Halibut Fillet with Ginger and Scallions

Cooking Time: 45 minutes

Serving Size: 4

Calories: 500

Ingredients:

- 3 scallions
- 2 tablespoons canola oil
- 4 tablespoons water
- 2 inches fresh ginger
- 1 tablespoon chicken powder
- 2 ½ pounds fillets
- ¼ teaspoon salt
- 2 teaspoons sugar

- 4 baby bok choy
- vegetable oil cooking spray
- 3 tablespoons lite soy sauce
- 4 Chinese black mushrooms
- ¼ teaspoon black pepper

Method:

1. Mix all ingredients in a processor and mix until lightly smooth.

2. Add eggs and blend again.

3. Steam fish fillets and place a lemon slice on each fillet.

4. Bring to boil water and steam for 3 to 4 minutes after the water starts boiling. Do not overcook.

5. Place fillets in a dish and pour the sauce over it. Cool at room temperature. Serve with spinach leaves.

Chapter 4: Chinese Lunch and Snack Recipes

4.1 Chinese Snack Recipes

Seasoned Snack Mix

Cooking Time: 30 minutes

Serving Size: 10

Calories: 450

Ingredients:

- ¼ cup Crisco Butter Flavor
- ¾ teaspoon garlic salt
- ¼ teaspoon cayenne pepper
- 2 cups oyster crackers
- 7 ounces peanuts
- ¾ cup grated Parmesan cheese
- salt

- ¼ teaspoon onion powder
- 3 cups of rice
- 2 teaspoons Worcestershire sauce
- 2 teaspoons Italian seasoning
- 1 square cereal
- 2 cups round toasted oat cereal
- 2 cups pretzel sticks

Method:

1. Preheat oven at 325°F.
2. Melt shortening in the oven and rest it aside.
3. Add Worcestershire sauce, seasoning, garlic, ginger, salt, and pepper in a bowl and stir.
4. Add other ingredients and melted shortenings into the mixture.
5. Mix well and spread evenly on the baking sheet.
6. Bake 16 to 18 minutes in oven and stir after 10 minutes.
7. Cool and store in containers.

Energy Snack Cake

Cooking Time: 85 minutes

Serving Size: 4

Calories: 920

Ingredients:

- 300 grams walnut pieces
- 100 grams flour
- 60 grams of dried cranberries
- 10 dried figs

- ½ teaspoon baking soda
- ¼ teaspoon baking powder
- 3 large eggs
- 15 grams of dried dates
- 80 grams of dried apricots
- ½ teaspoon salt
- 140 grams of sugar
- 1 teaspoon vanilla extract

Method:

1. Mix baking powder, baking soda, flour, and salt in a bowl.
2. Add nuts, dried fruits, and sugar in the mixture.
3. Heat oven to 150°F.
4. Take a small bowl and beat eggs with vanilla extract.
5. Add egg mixture into the flour mixture and mix well.
6. Add other ingredients and pour them into a baking pan.
7. Bake for 60 to 70 minutes.
8. Let it cool and cut into slices.

Taco Snack Mix

Cooking Time: 16 minutes

Serving Size: 4

Calories: 120

Ingredients:

- 2 cups crackers
- 2 cups of corn chips

- 2 cups Rice Chex Cereal
- 1 package McCormick Taco Seasoning Mix
- 2 cups Wheat Chex Cereal
- ½ cup unsalted butter

Method:

1. Microwave butter for 40 seconds until butter melts.
2. Take a bowl and mix cereals, corn chips, cheese crackers.
3. Add seasoning in the mixture and stir well.
4. Microwave mixture uncovered for 6 to 8 minutes until crispy.
5. Cool at room temperature.

One-Bowl Caramel Snack Cake with Caramel Glaze

Cooking Time: 60 minutes

Serving Size: 9

Calories: 610

Ingredients:

- ¾ cup cake flour
- 1 ½ teaspoons baking powder
- ¼ cup confectioners' sugar
- 1 large egg
- 2 large egg yolks
- cooking oil spray
- ¾ cup unsalted butter
- ¾ teaspoon salt

For cake:

- 1 cup dark brown sugar
- 1 cup heavy cream
- 1 tablespoon vanilla extract
- 1 cup all-purpose flour

For caramel:

- ½ cup heavy cream
- 1 teaspoon flaky sea salt
- 1 teaspoon vanilla extract
- 1 cup dark brown sugar

Method:

1. Heat oven at 350°F and Grease the pan with oil. Set aside.
2. Melt butter in the microwave oven and separate ¼ cup.
3. Add brown sugar and cream in remaining butter.
4. Microwave 1 minute and stir. Microwave for more 1 minute until caramel thickens. Set aside to cool down.
5. Use powder ingredients and mix them into the caramel.
6. Stir with a rubber spatula until combine.
7. Bake for 20 minutes on the middle rack.
8. Rotate baking pan and bake for more than 20 minutes until softens.
9. Pour remaining butter and caramel on the cake and set aside.
10. Let it cool down for 10 minutes and cut into pieces.

Snack Dippers with Hillshire Farm Smoked Sausage and Honey Mustard

Cooking Time: 35 minutes

Serving Size: 10

Calories: 170

Ingredients:

- 2 tablespoons yellow mustard
- 1 tablespoon honey
- ¼ cup packed brown sugar
- ¼ cup mayonnaise
- ¼ teaspoon black pepper
- 14 ounces Smoked Sausage

Method:

1. Place sausages in a tray and unwrap. Freeze for 30 minutes.
2. Use a cutting board to cut sausages into ¼ size pieces.
3. Heat oven to 325°F.
4. Transfer sausages in the baking dish and spread brown sugar.
5. Bake sausages for 20 minutes until lightly browned.
6. Mix other ingredients in a bowl and dip sausages to serve.

Afternoon Snack Muffins

Cooking Time: 65 minutes

Serving Size: 4

Calories: 760

Ingredients:

- 4 eggs
- 2 tablespoons chocolate sprinkles
- 1 container yogurt
- 200 grams flour
- 100 grams margarine
- 200 grams of sugar
- 1 teaspoon baking powder
- 1 handful walnuts

Method:

1. Heat oven to 180°C.
2. Grease muffin pan with butter and flour. Set aside.
3. Beat sugar and eggs until the mixture becomes fluffy.
4. Add yogurt and margarine. Beat again.
5. Add baking powder and flour. Beat again until it forms a smooth batter.
6. Add chocolate sprinkles and walnuts. Stir with a spoon.
7. Place dough in muffin cups and bake for 50 minutes.
8. Remove from the oven and let it cool down.

Wheat Bread Snack

Cooking Time: 10 minutes

Serving Size: 4

Calories: 90

Ingredients:

- watercress

- 1 slice whole-wheat bread
- olive oil
- 1 cup skimmed milk

Method:

1. Toast bread to a golden-brown color.
2. Pour watercress and olive oil on toast.
3. Serve with milk.

Apple Peanut Butter Snack

Cooking Time: 10 minutes

Serving Size: 2

Calories: 360

Ingredients:

- 2 tablespoons sunflower kernels
- ¼ cup Smucker's Peanut Butter
- 2 apples
- ¼ teaspoon ground cinnamon
- ¼ cup plain yogurt
- 1 tablespoon apple juice

Method:

1. Cut the apple into small slices.
2. Mix cinnamon, yogurt, peanut butter, apple juice, and kernels in processor and blend well.
3. Apply mixture evenly on sliced apples and let it cool down.

Honey Almond Snack Mix

Cooking Time: 15 minutes

Serving Size: 4

Calories: 320

Ingredients:

- 2 cups of cereal
- 2 cups of rice cereal squares
- 1 cup whole almonds
- ½ teaspoon salt
- ½ teaspoon ground red pepper
- ¼ cup Coconut Oil
- ¼ cup honey

Method:

1. Heat oven to 365°F.
2. Grease pan with baking paper and flour. Set aside.
3. Combine almonds, salt, pepper, and cereals in large bowls.
4. Take a small bowl and mix honey with coconut.
5. Pour in cereal mixture and stir well.
6. Spread into baking pan and bake for 15 to 18 minutes.
7. Let it cool and cut into slices.

Chinese BBQ Pork

Cooking Time: 20 minutes

Serving Size: 4

Calories: 352

Ingredients:

- 1 tablespoon honey
- 2 teaspoons fresh ginger root
- ½ cup dry sherry
- 8 drops red food coloring
- 2 pounds pork loin roast
- 1 teaspoon sesame oil
- 1 whole scallion
- 3 tablespoons soy sauce
- 2 ½ tablespoons hoisin sauce

Method:

1. Cut pork into small pieces.
2. Take a cooking bowl and grease with oil.
3. Place all ingredients in the cooker and mix.
4. Cover and cook for 7 hours on low heat.
5. Serve with fried rice.

Yam Bean, Carrot, and Cucumber Snack

Cooking Time: 45 minutes

Serving Size: 3

Calories: 260

Ingredients:

- Worcestershire sauce
- Peanuts
- 2 carrots
- ½ yam bean

- Unflavored gelatin
- Hot sauce
- Lime juice
- Japanese peanuts
- 1 cucumber
- 6 limes

Method:

1. Grate carrot, yam beans, and cucumber. Drain all thoroughly.
2. Grease baking pan with oil and pour beans.
3. Sprinkle gelatin and lime slices. Press firmly.
4. Add a layer of cucumber and carrots with the same process.
5. Cover and freeze for 30 minutes.
6. Mix other ingredients to make the sauce.
7. Sprinkle peanuts for garnish.

4.2 Chinese Lunch Recipes

These are some Chinese recipes that are common in the Chinese menu and easy to prepare with fewer ingredients.

Stir-Fried Tofu with Rice

Cooking Time: 40 minutes

Serving Size: 2

Calories: 281

Ingredients:

For the Tofu:

- 100 grams of tofu
- 1-inch ginger
- 3 Garlic cloves
- 1-inch red onion
- 1 Lemongrass stick
- 2 Shallots
- A handful of coriander leaves
- 1 teaspoon refined oil
- 2 teaspoon soya sauce

- 2 teaspoon chili paste
- 2 teaspoon honey

For the Fried Rice:

- 2 teaspoon soya sauce
- ½ Lemon
- Carrots
- Coriander leaves
- 1 teaspoon olive oil
- Spring onions
- Salt and pepper
- 1 Fresh red chilly
- 1 Ginger

Method:

1. Add chopped mariner in a preheated pan and stir well.
2. Add seasonings, garlic, shallots, and ginger.
3. Add honey, soy sauce, and chili paste.
4. Add coriander and mix with a rubber spatula. Set aside.
5. Mix carrot, onion, salt, pepper, and ginger in a pan.
6. Drizzle in oil then add chili, lemon juice, and soy sauce.
7. Add coriander in cooked rice and cook for 7 more minutes.
8. Serve rice.

Dim Sums

Cooking Time: 1 hour 20 minutes

Serving Size: 4

Calories: 237

Ingredients:

For Chicken and Prawn Dumplings:

- 5 ml sesame oil
- 2.5 grams white pepper
- 150 grams of chicken
- Wonton skin
- Potato starch
- 150 grams prawn
- 5 grams of sugar
- Salt

For Vegetable Coriander Dumplings:

- 10 grams of water chestnuts
- 10 grams of carrots
- 10 grams button mushrooms
- 5 grams of sugar
- 10 grams garlic
- 10 grams of bamboo shoots
- 5 grams sesame oil
- 10 ml of oil
- 10 grams brown garlic

For Wonton Skin:

- Salt
- 50 grams of wheat starch
- Potato starch

Method:

1. Mix prawns and chicken with salt, potato starch, sesame oil, and sugar.

2. Stuff wanton skin in mixture and steam. Serve with soya sauce.

3. For dumplings, mix all ingredients except wanton skin.

4. Stuff mixture in wanton skin and steam. Serve with sauce.

5. To prepare wanton skin, add potato in wheat starch, salt, and water.

6. Add potato starch and stir till tightens.

7. Cut into pieces and roll balls. Add fillings.

8. For the sauce, fry garlic in oil. Soak chilies and make a paste.

9. Add chili paste when garlic gets brown. Add seasonings.

Hot and Sour Soup

Cooking Time: 1 hour 15 minutes

Serving Size: 4

Calories: 39

Ingredients:

- 1 ½ tablespoon vinegar
- Salt
- 60 grams prawns
- 1 tablespoon soya sauce
- ½ tablespoon chili powder
- 5 grams of carrot

- 5 grams of cabbage
- 1 Egg
- 1 tablespoon coriander
- 1 teaspoon chili oil
- 5 grams of bamboo shoots
- 5 grams black mushrooms
- 5 grams button mushrooms
- 100 grams of chicken
- ½ teaspoon white pepper
- 2 tablespoon corn flour
- 5 grams of bean sprouts
- 5 grams of fresh beans
- 2 cups stock

Method:

1. Cut all vegetables, prawns, and chickens into small pieces.
2. Cook all vegetables with chicken in a wok.
3. Add seasonings and other remaining ingredients into wok.
4. Add corn flour and egg in the end to a thick soup.

Quick Noodles

Cooking Time: 45 minutes

Serving Size: 2

Calories: 188

Ingredients:

- 1 cup carrot, julienne

- 1 tablespoon vegetable oil
- 1 cup onion
- 1 cup spring onions
- 2 packets noodles
- 1 tablespoon ginger and garlic chili paste
- 1 tablespoon coriander
- 1 tablespoon lemon juice
- 1 teaspoon vinegar
- 1 tablespoon soy sauce
- 1 tablespoon Schezuan sauce
- 1 cup pepper
- 1 cup mushrooms
- ½ lettuce
- ½ teaspoon turmeric powder
- 1 teaspoon sugar

Method:

1. Cook noodles using instructions on the pack. Drain and cool in the water.
2. Add oil in noodles and mix to avoid sticking noodles with each other.
3. Heat oil in a wok.
4. Mix vegetables and soya sauce, mushroom, ginger, and garlic paste and fry in wok.
5. Mix remaining ingredients in a small bowl and stir.
6. Add this mixture to vegetable mixture and add noodles. Mix well.

7. Garnish with chopped coriander and serve.

Szechuan Chili Chicken

Cooking Time: 45 minutes

Serving Size: 8

Calories: 179

Ingredients:

- 3 tablespoon brown peppercorn
- Salt
- 2-3 spring onions
- 2 teaspoon white pepper
- 5-6 dry red chilies
- 2-3 tablespoon ginger
- 3 tablespoon green peppercorn
- 10-12 pieces chicken
- 1 tablespoon black vinegar
- 2 teaspoon chili oil
- oil for frying

Method:

1. Fry chicken with ginger until color changes to brown.
2. Drain oil and set it aside.
3. Add onion, garlic, peppercorn, and brown peppercorn.
4. Sauté for 5 minutes and add spices.
5. Stir for more than 10 minutes and add black vinegar.
6. Fry for more than 10 minutes and garnish with peppercorns.

Shitake Fried Rice with Water Chestnuts

Cooking Time: 25 minutes

Serving Size: 2

Calories: 291

Ingredients:

- 1 Cup Shitake mushroom
- 1 tablespoon Ginger
- A pinch of White pepper
- 1 big drop Sesame oil
- 1 cup rice (cooked)
- Green chilies
- 2-3 tablespoon Vegetable oil
- 4 cloves garlic
- 2-3 Water chestnuts
- 1 big tablespoon Celery
- ½ Medium Onion
- 1 big tablespoon Leeks
- Small bunch Parsley
- A dash of Rice wine vinegar
- 1 big drop of Sesame oil
- Salt to season
- 1 stalk Spring onions

Method:

1. Slice mushrooms, chestnuts, and green chilies.
2. Heat wok and add 1 tablespoon vegetable oil.

3. Add celery, onion, and leeks in oil.

4. Add mushrooms, chestnuts, and ginger.

5. Add rice, onion, sauces, and other ingredients.

6. Stir fry and put into the bowl.

Chicken with Chestnuts

Cooking Time: 45 minutes

Serving Size: 4

Calories: 294

Ingredients:

- 5 dried Chinese mushrooms
- 1 tablespoon fish sauce
- 1 tablespoon date puree
- 1 diced green capsicum
- 2 tablespoon sesame oil
- ½ kg chicken mince
- 1 diced red capsicum
- 3 tablespoon white radish
- 50 ml of water
- ½ teaspoon chili flakes
- 12-14 peeled water chestnuts
- 2 tablespoon chopped spring onion
- 1 tablespoon chopped garlic
- 1 tablespoon vinegar
- 1 iceberg lettuce
- 1 tablespoon shredded ginger

- 1 tablespoon soya sauce
- 1 tablespoon chopped coriander

Method:

1. Soak mushrooms in boiling water for 30 minutes and discard stems of mushrooms.
2. Heat oil in wok and fry chicken with ginger until lightly browned.
3. Fry ginger, garlic, and capsicum for 3 minutes.
4. Put the chicken into pan and heat.
5. Add remaining ingredients into chicken except for lettuce and coriander.
6. Add vegetables and mix well.
7. Serve with lettuce and garnish with coriander leaves.

Honey Chili Potato

Cooking Time: 35 minutes

Serving Size: 2

Calories: 586

Ingredients:

For Frying Potatoes:

- 5 tablespoon Corn flour
- 2 Potatoes
- 1 ½ tablespoon Salt
- 2 teaspoon Chili Powder

For Honey Chili Sauce:

- 4 teaspoon Sesame Seeds
- 2 tablespoon Honey

- 1 teaspoon Chili Flakes
- 2 Bulbs Spring Onions
- 1 ½ teaspoon Garlic
- 1 teaspoon Vinegar
- 2 teaspoon Tomato Sauce
- 2 teaspoon Chili Sauce
- 1 teaspoon Ginger
- 2 Whole Red Chilies
- 1 teaspoon salt

Method:

1. Take 2 potatoes and cut them into lengthwise slices.
2. Rinse them with water and soak for 15 minutes.
3. Add slices into a bowl and put some salt, corn flour, chili, and coriander leaves.
4. Mix well until sticky.
5. Take a frying pan and heat 3 tablespoon oil.
6. Fry potatoes into the oil until golden brown and crispy.
7. Do not fry on high flame as it can cause potatoes to burn from the outer side and uncooked from the inner side.
8. When cooked properly, set aside.
9. Take another frying pan and put sesame seeds to heat until golden brown. Set aside.
10. Heat oil in a pan and add chili flakes, tomato sauce, ginger, garlic, and red chilies.
11. Stir well and add vinegar, chili sauce, honey, and salt.
12. Stir and make the sauce.

13. Add fried potatoes in sauce and mix well.

14. Serve potatoes with juice.

Peri-Peri Chicken Satay

Cooking Time: 25 minutes

Serving Size: 2

Calories: 104

Ingredients:

- 50 grams Peri-Peri sauce
- 100 grams of potato fries
- 100 grams of yogurt
- 200 grams of chicken thigh
- salt and pepper
- 5 grams of chili powder
- Oil to fry
- 25 grams ginger garlic paste
- 5 grams coriander leaves

Method:

1. Soak skewers for 60 minutes.
2. Add ginger, garlic, salt, pepper, Peri-Peri sauce, chili, and garlic in a bowl.
3. Mix well and add chicken.
4. Marinate for 2 hours in a sealing bag.
5. Heat grill on medium heat.
6. Place chicken on grill and brush with oil to prevent sticking.
7. Grill for 15 to 20 minutes until brown.

8. Serve chicken with crispy potato fries.

Cantonese Chicken Soup

Cooking Time: 40 minutes

Serving Size: 2

Calories: 132

Ingredients:

- 5 spoons large chicken stock
- 10 Mushrooms
- 1 whole chicken
- 5 Pieces bok choy
- 3-4 spring onions

Method:

1. Cut chicken skin and piece chicken into large slices about 10 to 12.
2. Cut mushrooms into halves.
3. Take a container and layer bok choy, mushrooms, and chicken evenly.
4. Add chicken stock and cook for an hour.
5. Add remaining ingredients and water as your requirement.
6. Cook for more than 20 minutes.
7. Use corn flour to give thickness to the soup.

Vegetable Manchow Soup

Cooking Time: 35 minutes

Serving Size: 2

Calories: 128.8

Ingredients:

- 2 tablespoon French beans
- 2 tablespoon Carrots
- 2 Spring onions
- 1 teaspoon Pepper
- 4 Cups Water
- 2 tablespoon Mushrooms
- 1 teaspoon Ginger
- 1 teaspoon Garlic
- 1 teaspoon Green chilies
- 2 stems Spring onion
- Oil and salt
- 1 tablespoon Coriander leaves
- 2 tablespoon Cabbage
- 1 tablespoon Soya sauce
- 4 tablespoon Corn flour
- 1 cup Water
- 2 tablespoon Capsicum

Method:

1. Stir fry coriander leaves, garlic, green chilies, and ginger for 2 minutes.

2. Cut all vegetables and add them into the ginger-garlic mixture.

3. Add seasonings and sauces. Fry for more than 5 minutes.

4. Add water and wait until it starts boiling.

5. Take a small bowl and mix corn flour in hot water.

6. Add corn flour mixture into boiling water and vegetable mixture.

7. Stir until it starts thickening.

8. Remove from heat and garnish with green onions.

Garlic Soya Chicken

Cooking Time: 35 minutes

Serving Size: 2

Calories: 119.3

Ingredients:

- ¼ teaspoon White Pepper
- 1 teaspoon Ginger Juice
- 450 Gram Chicken Breast
- 1 teaspoon Sesame Oil
- 1 tablespoon ginger, grated
- 1 tablespoon Rice Vinegar
- 2 tablespoon Vegetable oil
- A handful of Snow Peas
- 2 tablespoon Soy Sauce
- 5-6 Garlic cloves
- ½ Cup Red Onion
- 1 teaspoon Red Chili Flakes
- ½ Red Bell Pepper

For the Sauce:

- 2 teaspoon Chinese Rice Wine

- ½ tablespoon Brown Sugar
- 1 teaspoon Corn flour
- 2 teaspoon Dark Soy Sauce

Method:

1. Cut chicken into small pieces.
2. Take a large bowl and mix chicken with sesame oil and white pepper.
3. Marinate chicken for 15 to 20 minutes.
4. Take a small bowl and mix all ingredients of sauces and mix well.
5. Put a frying pan on low heat. Add 2 tablespoon oil and spread it into a frying pan.
6. Gradually add chicken pieces into the frying pan and wait for 5 minutes.
7. The flame should be low. Wait until chicken sides turn into light brown color.
8. Stir chicken until all sides turn brown and remove immediately from the frying pan.
9. Turn the heat up and fry peas and red onion for 1 minute.
10. Stir continuously to prevent burning or overheating.
11. Add bell pepper and cook for one more minute.
12. Mix all ingredients well and when vegetables get crispy, stir in chicken.
13. Make sauce ingredients and cook on low heat until sticky and smooth.
14. Pour sauce on chicken and vegetables.

15. Add 1 tablespoon water and cook for 2 minutes until bubbly and thick.

16. Serve with fried rice and lettuce.

Chapter 5: Chinese Dinner and Dessert Recipes

5.1 Dinner Recipes of Chinese Cuisine

Shrimp Fried Rice

Cooking Time: 20 minutes

Serving Size: 6

Calories: 332

Ingredients:

- 1 package frozen mixed vegetables
- 1-pound medium shrimp
- 4 tablespoons butter
- 4 large eggs
- ¼ teaspoon pepper
- 8 bacon strips

- 3 cups cold cooked rice
- ½ teaspoon salt

Method:

1. Take a large skillet and heat on low flame.
2. Add 1 tablespoon vegetable oil or butter.
3. Beat eggs and pour into skillet.
4. Stir to cook on all sides. Remove from skillet and set aside.
5. Melt butter in the skillet again and add vinegar.
6. Add cooked rice and shrimp into the skillet.
7. Stir and cook for 5 minutes until shrimp color changes to pink.
8. Cut eggs into pieces and add in skillet. Cook on low flame.
9. Remove from flame after 5 minutes and garnish with coriander leaves.

Ginger-Cashew Chicken Salad

Cooking Time: 30 minutes

Serving Size: 8

Calories: 379

Ingredients:

- ¼ teaspoon cayenne pepper
- 4 boneless skinless chicken breast halves
- ½ cup cider vinegar
- 2 teaspoons reduced-sodium soy sauce
- 1 teaspoon salt

- ½ cup molasses
- ½ cup canola oil
- 2 tablespoons minced fresh gingerroot

For Salad:

- 2 tablespoons sesame seeds
- 1 can mandarin oranges
- 1 cup shredded red cabbage
- 3 green onions
- 2 cups Chow Mein noodles
- 8 ounces fresh baby spinach
- ¾ cup salted cashews
- 2 medium carrots

Method:

1. Blend all ingredients in a processor except chicken.
2. Add chicken in a bowl and pour processed ingredients over it.
3. Mix and marinate chicken for 3 hours.
4. Heat the broiler and put the chicken into it.
5. Boil for 20 minutes. Change sides and boil for 15 more minutes.
6. Cut the ingredients of salad and make noodles.
7. Add chicken in a separate dish, add salad and noodles. Serve with sauce.

Beef and Spinach Lo Mein

Cooking Time: 30 minutes

Serving Size: 5

Calories: 363

Ingredients:

- 1 tablespoon water
- 4 teaspoons canola oil
- 1 can sliced water chestnuts
- ¼ cup hoisin sauce
- 2 tablespoons soy sauce
- 1-pound beef top round steak
- 1 package fresh spinach
- 1 red chili pepper
- 6 ounces Spaghetti
- 2 teaspoons sesame oil
- 2 garlic cloves
- ¼ teaspoon crushed red pepper flakes
- 2 green onions

Method:

1. Mix hoisin, soy sauce, garlic, pepper, sesame oil, and water.
2. Separate ¼ cup of mixture in a large bowl.
3. Add beef in this mixture and mix well. Marinate for 10 minutes at room temperature.
4. Prepare spaghetti and follow package directions.
5. Take a skillet and heat it. Add canola oil.
6. Add the beef mixture in parts. Do not load the skillet with the whole mix.

7. Stir-fry beef mixture until pink. Remove and repeat with remaining mixture.

8. Heat a skillet and add remaining ingredients and hoisin mixture.

9. Cook for 15 minutes. Add beef mixture.

10. Add spaghetti and mix well. Cook for 5 minutes and serve hot.

Ginger Pork Lettuce Wraps

Cooking Time: 30 minutes

Serving Size: 2 dozen

Calories: 54

Ingredients:

- 1 tablespoon sesame oil
- 24 Boston lettuce leaves
- 1-pound lean ground pork
- 1 can sliced water chestnuts
- 4 green onions
- 1 medium onion
- ¼ cup hoisin sauce
- 1 tablespoon red wine vinegar
- 1 tablespoon reduced-sodium soy sauce
- 2 teaspoons Thai chili sauce
- 4 garlic cloves
- 1 tablespoon fresh ginger root

Method:

1. Take a large skillet and cook onion with pork for 10 minutes.

2. Remove when the pink color disappears, and onions become tender.

3. Cut into pieces and make crumbles.

4. Blend soy sauce, vinegar, garlic, ginger, and hoisin sauce.

5. Add remaining ingredients and heat for 10 minutes.

6. Place pork on lettuce leaves and mixture over it. Fold and serve.

Mushroom Pepper Steak

Cooking Time: 30 minutes

Serving Size: 4

Calories: 241

Ingredients:

- 1 cup julienned green pepper
- ½ teaspoon minced fresh ginger root
- 1-pound beef top sirloin steak
- 2 medium tomatoes
- 2 cups sliced fresh mushrooms
- 3 teaspoons canola oil
- 1 cup julienned sweet red pepper
- 6 tablespoons reduced-sodium soy sauce
- ¼ teaspoon pepper
- 1 garlic clove

- 6 green onions
- Hot cooked rice
- 1 tablespoon cornstarch
- ½ cup reduced-sodium beef broth

Method:

1. Take a bowl and mix salt, vinegar.
2. Add beef and mix well.
3. Marinate in the refrigerator for 30 to 60 minutes.
4. Take a small bowl and mix corn starch, soy sauce, and remaining broth.
5. Mix until smooth. Set aside.
6. Heat a skillet and add ginger, garlic in vegetable oil.
7. Add beef and discard the remaining marinade.
8. Stir fry beef in oil until no longer pink.
9. Remove from heat and set aside. Keep warm.
10. Stir fry mushrooms, vegetables with remaining ingredients and broth.
11. Add beef and mix well.
12. Cook for 10 minutes and serve with rice.

Asparagus Beef Sauté

Cooking Time: 30 minutes

Serving Size: 4

Calories: 328

Ingredients:

- 1-pound fresh asparagus
- 1 tablespoon canola oil

- 2 garlic cloves
- 1 green onion
- ½ teaspoon salt
- 1 ½ teaspoon lemon juice
- Hot cooked rice
- ½ pound sliced fresh mushrooms
- 1-pound beef tenderloin (¾ -inch cubes)
- ¼ teaspoon pepper
- ¼ cup butter
- 1 tablespoon reduced-sodium soy sauce

Method:

1. Mix salt and pepper with beef.
2. Take a frying pan and add 1 tablespoon cooking oil into it.
3. Add garlic and ginger. Stir fry for 2 minutes.
4. Add beef and fry for 10 minutes until lightly brown.
5. Remove from pan and set aside. Keep warm.
6. Add 1 tablespoon oil in the same skillet and put mushrooms.
7. Add asparagus and cook until tender. Add remaining ingredients and cook for 10 more minutes.
8. Add beef. Heat for 2 minutes and remove. Set aside and serve with rice.

Beef Orange Stir-Fry

Cooking Time: 25 minutes

Serving Size: 2

Calories: 390

Ingredients:

- ¼ cup of orange juice
- 2 teaspoons oil
- 3 cups vegetable (stir-fry)
- 1 tablespoon cornstarch
- 1 tablespoon soy sauce
- 1 garlic clove
- 1 cup hot cooked rice
- ½ pound beef sirloin steak
- ½ teaspoon sesame oil
- red flakes (pepper)
- ¼ cup of cold water

Method:

1. Take a small bowl and combine cornstarch, water, orange juice, soy sauce, pepper flakes, and sesame oil.
2. Stir until smooth. Set aside.
3. Heat wok and add 1 tablespoon vegetable oil. Add beef and heat.
4. Stir fry until golden brown.
5. Stir fry vegetables and cornstarch mixture in a skillet.
6. Add beef and other ingredients. Cook for 2 minutes and serve with rice.

Speedy Salmon Stir-Fry

Cooking Time: 30 minutes

Serving Size: 4

Calories: 498

Ingredients:

- 1 package frozen stir-fry vegetable blend
- 1 tablespoon molasses
- 1 tablespoon reduced-sodium soy sauce
- 1-pound salmon fillets
- 1 teaspoon grated orange zest
- 4 teaspoons canola oil
- 2 cups hot cooked brown rice
- 1 tablespoon sesame seeds
- 1 tablespoon minced fresh ginger root
- ¼ cup reduced-fat honey mustard salad dressing
- 2 tablespoons orange juice

Method:

1. Take a small bowl and mix honey, ginger, mustard, soy sauce, orange zest, and molasses.

2. Heat 2 tablespoon oil in the skillet and add salmon and cook for 5 to 7 minutes until fish becomes soft.

3. In a small frying pan, add oil. Heat and add vegetable mixture, salad dressings, and remaining ingredients.

4. Add salmon and stir gently.

5. Sprinkle sesame seeds and serve with rice.

Asian Glazed Chicken Thighs

Cooking Time: 25 minutes

Serving Size: 4

Calories: 274

Ingredients:

- 4 boneless skinless chicken thighs
- 3 garlic cloves, minced
- ¼ cup of rice vinegar
- ½ teaspoon ground ginger
- Toasted sesame seeds
- 2 teaspoons canola oil
- 3 tablespoons reduced-sodium soy sauce
- 2 tablespoons honey

Method:

1. Take a small bowl and blend honey, soy sauce, and vinegar.
2. In a large skillet, add 1 tablespoon of oil. Add chicken and heat until brown on each side.
3. Add blended mixture and heat for 2 minutes.
4. Add remaining ingredients and cook until it starts boiling.
5. Add in a dish and sprinkle sesame seeds. Serve with rice.

Mandarin Pork Stir-Fry

Cooking Time: 25 minutes

Serving Size: 4

Calories: 473

Ingredients:

- ½ teaspoon garlic powder
- 1 pork tenderloin (cut into 2-inch strips)

- ½ teaspoon ground ginger
- 2 tablespoons soy sauce
- 2 cups uncooked instant rice
- ½ cup of orange juice
- 1 package frozen sugar snap peas
- 1 can mandarin oranges, drained
- ¼ cup of water
- 1 tablespoon cornstarch
- 2 tablespoons canola oil

Method:

1. Follow package direction and cook rice according to these directions.
2. Take a bowl and mix garlic, ginger, and cornstarch.
3. Add orange juice and stir. Add soy sauce and water.
4. Mix until smooth and set aside.
5. Take a large skillet and add 1 tablespoon oil.
6. Add pork and stir fry until lightly brown. Set aside.
7. Add peas in the same skillet and boil until tender.
8. Add orange mixture and pork in skillet.
9. Stir fry for 2 minutes and remove. Serve with rice.

Hoisin-Pineapple Salmon

Cooking Time: 20 minutes

Serving Size: 4

Calories: 349

Ingredients:

- ¼ teaspoon pepper

- ½ cup unsweetened crushed pineapple
- 4 salmon fillets
- ¼ cup orange marmalade
- 2 tablespoons chopped fresh cilantro
- 2 tablespoons hoisin sauce

Method:

1. Heat oven at 400°F.
2. Prepare baking pan and grease with oil. Spread salmon and hoisin sauce.
3. Bake for 15 to 20 minutes or when fish begins to flake.
4. Take a small saucepan and mix pineapple with orange marmalade.
5. Bring to boil and stir continuously.
6. Pour over salmon and sprinkle coriander leaves.

Tropical Sweet and Spicy Pork Tenderloin

Cooking Time: 30 minutes

Serving Size: 4

Calories: 539

Ingredients:

- 2 finely chopped chipotle peppers
- 2 tablespoons olive oil
- 1 medium onion, chopped
- 1 medium green pepper, chopped
- 1 pork tenderloin cut into 1-inches cubes
- 3 garlic cloves, minced
- 1 cup chicken stock

- 1 can pineapple tidbits, drained
- ¼ teaspoon salt
- ¼ teaspoon pepper
- 2 tablespoons reduced-sodium soy sauce
- Hot cooked rice
- ½ cup packed brown sugar
- 1 cup honey barbecue sauce
- 2 teaspoons adobo sauce

Method:

1. Take a large skillet. Heat and add oil.
2. Sprinkle salt and pepper on pork and stir fry for 5 to 7 minutes.
3. Remove when cooked from both sides.
4. Take a pan and add ginger, garlic, chicken stock, onion.
5. Stir for 3 minutes.
6. Add remaining ingredients and cook for 5 minutes.
7. Add pork and cook until tender.
8. Remove and serve with rice.

5.2 Chinese Desserts Recipes

Chinese Almond Cookies

Cooking Time: 40 minutes

Serving Size: 30

Calories: 660

Ingredients:

- ½ teaspoon baking soda

- 2 cups flour
- ½ teaspoon baking powder
- ¼ teaspoon salt
- 2 ½ teaspoons almond extract
- 30 whole almonds
- ½ cup shortening
- ¾ cup white sugar
- 1 egg
- ½ cup butter
- 1 egg beaten

Method:

1. Heat Oven at 325°F.
2. Take a large bowl and add flour.
3. Add salt and mix well.
4. Add baking soda and baking powder. Stir well.
5. In a small bowl, beat butter, shortening, and sugar.
6. Add almond and egg in butter mixture and blend well.
7. Add flour mixture and blend until smooth.
8. Knead the dough and cut into 2 pieces.
9. Refrigerate for 2 hours.
10. Cut the dough into 14 to 15 pieces lengthwise.
11. Grease cookie tray and roll each piece in the round motion.
12. Put round balls into a cookie tray and add almonds in the center of each ball.
13. Grease cookies with beaten egg using a brush.

14. Bake for 15 to 20 minutes until golden brown.

15. Remove and let it cool. Serve when cold and crispy.

Nian Gao

Cooking Time: 60 minutes

Serving Size: 10

Calories: 338

Ingredients:

- 2 ½ cups milk

- One can red azuki beans

- 16 ounces mochiko sweet rice flour

- 1 to 1 ¾ cup sugar

- 1 tablespoon baking soda

- ½ cup unsalted butter

- ¾ cup of vegetable oil

- 3 eggs

Method:

1. Heat oven at 350°F.

2. Grease pan with butter or oil using spray or brush.

3. Mix all ingredients except beans in a processor and blend until smooth.

4. Sprinkle mochiko flour on the baking dish and add half batter.

5. Spread beans on top and add another layer of remaining batter on beans.

6. Bake for 40 to 45 minutes until cooked.

7. Check by using a toothpick if baked well.

8. Serve cold.

Eight Treasure Rice Pudding

Cooking Time: 105 minutes

Serving Size: 8

Calories: 432

Ingredients:

For the Rice:

- 1 cup black raisins
- 1 cup yellow raisins
- ¼ teaspoon salt

For the Fruit:

- Neutral oil for coating bowl
- 2 cups glutinous rice
- 1 tablespoon sunflower oil
- 1 cup sugar-glazed cherries
- 1 dried apricot

For the Filling:

- 1 cup sugar lotus seeds
- 100 grams red bean paste

For the Starch Water:

- 3 tablespoons water
- 2 teaspoon potato starch

For the Sugar Syrup:

- 1 tablespoon honey
- 1 tablespoon sugar

- ½ cup of water

Method:

1. Take a large bowl and put rice in it.

2. Add cold water and cover for 1 hour.

3. Drain and soak rice and steam for 40 minutes in simmering water.

4. Add oil and salt. Combine gently to prevent breaking rice.

5. Cut fruits in small pieces.

6. Take a bowl and grease with oil.

7. Add fruits and a layer of rice. Press gently.

8. Add red bean paste on it and spread with a spoon.

9. Place rice and cherries layer again.

10. Place the bowl in simmering water and steam for 30 minutes.

11. Take a small bowl and mix potato starch water ingredients.

12. Stir until well combined.

13. Place all syrup ingredients and bring to boil. Add starch water and boil for 10 minutes.

14. Remove the bowl from the water and invert it into the dish. Add sugary syrup on top.

Chinese Almond Float Dessert

Cooking Time: 60 minutes

Serving Size: 6

Calories: 312

Ingredients:

- 1 cup of cold water
- 1 can fruit cocktail with syrup
- 1 envelope unflavored gelatin
- 2 teaspoons almond extract
- 1 cup evaporated milk
- 4 tablespoons granulated sugar
- 1 cup boiling water

Method:

1. Take a small bowl and mix sugar with gelatin. Mix well.
2. Add boiling water in the gelatin mixture and stir continuously until dissolved.
3. Add almond extract, milk, and cold water. Mix well.
4. Wait until cool down. Cut into pieces and serve with can fruit.

Candied Banana Fritters

Cooking Time: 30 minutes

Serving Size: 4

Calories: 634

Ingredients:

- 3 to 6 tablespoons white sesame seeds
- ¾ cup of water
- 4 cups oil for deep-frying
- 1 egg, lightly beaten
- 1 cup all-purpose flour

- 5 bananas, firm
- 1 ½ cups granulated sugar
- 2 tablespoons oil

Method:

1. Cut bananas in small pieces about 1 ½ inch.
2. Combine water, egg, and flour. Stir and make the batter.
3. Heat oil in the frying pan. Take a banana slice and dip into the batter.
4. Carefully dip all slices and add them into hot oil for deep frying.
5. Fry until looks golden brown and batter is crispy.
6. Take a bowl and add cold water with ice cubes. Put it into the freezer.
7. Heat oil and add sugar. Stir until golden brown. Avoid high flame. It can cause sugar to burn.
8. Remove the wok and put it into cold water.
9. Use a stick to coat banana slices in syrup and add immediately into cold water until syrup is hardened.
10. Place in a dish and repeat with all slices.

Chinese Bow Tie Dessert with Honey and Brown Sugar

Cooking Time: 35 minutes

Serving Size: 16

Calories: 119

Ingredients:

- 4 to 6 cups oil
- 1 package egg roll wrappers

For the Syrup:

- ½ cup honey
- 1 cup brown sugar
- ½ cup of corn syrup
- ½ cup of water

Method:

1. Cut egg roll wrappers into four equal pieces.
2. Use 2 knives and make a knot like a bow tie on wrappers.
3. Heat wok and then add oil.
4. Fry bow tie for 5 minutes.
5. Boil syrup ingredients for 5 minutes.
6. Dip bow tie in sugar syrup and set aside.

Five-Spice Peanuts

Cooking Time: 40 minutes

Serving Size: 8

Calories: 266

Ingredients:

- 1 tablespoon light corn syrup
- 2 tablespoons butter
- ¼ cup brown sugar
- ½ teaspoon five-spice powder
- 2 cups unsalted peanuts

Method:

1. Take a baking tray and grease with oil.
2. In a large pan, melt butter, syrup, and sugar.

3. Heat on low flame and add five spices powder. Stir well.

4. Boil for 5 minutes and do not stir when it starts boiling.

5. Add on the baking sheet and mix peanuts. Wait to cool down and harden.

6. Cut into pieces and serve cold.

Chinese Sponge Cake

Cooking Time: 40 minutes

Serving Size: 3

Calories: 468

Ingredients:

- ½ tsp. cream of tartar
- ¾ cup sugar
- 1 cupcake flour
- 5 eggs
- 1 tsp. Baking powder
- ¼ tsp. salt
- 1 tsp. almond extract

Method:

1. Prepare pan and wok for steam.

2. Take a large bowl and mix flour, salt, baking powder, and baking soda. Stir well.

3. Take a bowl and separate egg whites from egg yolks. Beat egg whites until fluffy. Add cream and beat.

4. Add ¼ cup of sugar and beat again for 1 minute.

5. Add egg yolk in remaining sugar. Beat for 2 minutes and add almond extract.

6. Gradually add the egg mixture into the flour mixture.

7. Mix with a rubber spatula and set aside.

8. Pour batter into pan and heat wok.

9. Add water in the wok. Wait until it starts boiling.

10. Turn flame to medium and steam cake for 20 to 25 minutes covered.

11. Invert in the plate and cut into pieces.

Dairy-Free Mango Pudding

Cooking Time: 20 minutes

Serving Size: 4

Calories: 259

Ingredients:

- ¼ cup white sugar
- 1 cup good-quality coconut milk
- 1 packet gelatin
- 2 medium to large ripe mangoes
- ½ cup hot water

Method:

1. Take ripe mangoes and peel.

2. Blend mangoes in a processor until smooth. Set aside.

3. Take a pan and add water. Bring to boil.

4. Gradually add gelatin in water. Add milk and sugar.

5. Stir and blend with mango mixture.

6. Pour in a bowl and refrigerate for 2 hours.

Delicious Chinese Raspberry Snowflake Cake

Cooking Time: 25 minutes

Serving Size: 1 cake

Calories: 330

Ingredients:

Raspberry Snowflake Cake

- 450 milliliters water
- 125 grams of potato starch or corn flour
- 3 tablespoons desiccated coconut
- 55 grams raspberries
- 60 milliliters double cream
- 5 leaves gelatin
- 200 grams of sugar
- 200 milliliters whole milk

Coconut Milk Snowflake Cake

- 5 leaves gelatin
- 250 milliliters coconut milk
- 60 milliliters double cream
- 3 tablespoons desiccated coconut
- 125 grams of potato starch or corn flour
- 450 milliliters water
- 200 grams caster sugar

Method:

1. Take a small saucepan and cook water, raspberry, and sugar.

2. Keep whisking until boil and raspberry completely dissolve in sugar.

3. Let it cool down.

4. Add double cream and milk into raspberry jam and bring to boil.

5. Rest aside for 10 minutes and add gelatin. Stir well.

6. Add starch and 100ml additional water.

7. Prepare a baking tray and put mixture.

8. Keep in the refrigerator for 3 hours.

9. Slice and sprinkle coconut. Serve cold.

Fortune Cookies

Cooking Time: 30 minutes

Serving Size: 10

Calories: 133

Ingredients:

- 3 tablespoons vegetable oil
- 8 tablespoons sugar
- ½ teaspoon almond extract
- 3 teaspoons water
- 8 tablespoons all-purpose flour
- 2 large egg whites
- ½ teaspoon vanilla extract
- 1 ½ teaspoons cornstarch
- ¼ teaspoon salt

Method:

1. Heat oven at 300°F.

2. Beat egg, vanilla and almond extract, and vegetable oil in a bowl.

3. Take a large bowl and mix starch, flour, and water. Blend until smooth.

4. Add egg mixture into the flour mixture and blend to make the batter.

5. Grease baking pan with sheet and oil. Add batter with a spoon on sheet.

6. Put that paper in the middle of the cookies and fold edges.

7. Bake for 14 to 16 minutes until brown and crispy.

Chapter 6: Chinese Traditional Wok Recipes and Vegetarian Chinese Meals

6.1 Chinese Famous Wok Recipes

Spicy Oyster Sauce Squid with Green Peppers

Cooking Time: 15 minutes

Serving Size: 2

Calories: 512

Ingredients:

- 1 tablespoon low-sodium light soy sauce
- 1 green pepper (sliced into cubes)
- ½ teaspoon dark soy sauce
- 1 teaspoon oyster sauce
- 1 tablespoon rapeseed oil
- 1 medium white onion (cut into slices)

- 1 tablespoon fresh lemon juice
- A pinch of caster sugar
- 1 red chili (finely chopped)
- 200g whole baby squid (sliced into rings)
- 1 tablespoon rice vinegar

Method:

1. Heat wok and add 1 tablespoon oil.
2. Add sliced onion and rapeseed oil. Heat for 20 minutes until brown and crispy.
3. Add squid and red chili. Heat for 10 seconds. Add rice vinegar.
4. Add green pepper and stir for 1 minute.
5. Add 1 tablespoon water around the edges of the wok to create steam.
6. Cook for 1 minute more and add remaining ingredients.
7. Stir and serve immediately.

Vegetarian Hokkien Mee

Cooking Time: 22 minutes

Serving Size: 2

Calories: 522

Ingredients:

- A knob of fresh ginger (grated)
- 100g Quorn mince
- 1 tablespoon low-sodium light soy sauce
- A drizzle of toasted sesame oil

- 1 tablespoon rapeseed oil
- 2 garlic cloves (chopped)
- 1 teaspoon dark soy sauce
- 2 mini sweet shallots (chopped)
- 1 red chili (chopped)
- 400g cooked egg noodles (200g dried)
- 100g fresh beansprouts
- 3 dried Chinese mushrooms (soaked and finely diced)
- 100ml hot vegetable stock

For Garnish

- Spring onions (sliced)
- Red chili, (sliced into rings)

Method:

1. Heat wok on high flame. Add the rapeseed oil and stir.
2. Add garlic, ginger, chili, and shallots.
3. Heat and stir to explode flavors in the wok for 1 minute.
4. Add dark soy sauce, mushroom, and Quorn. Leave for 2 minutes.
5. Add soy sauce and vegetable stock. Cook for 10 minutes.
6. Add cooked egg noodles and spread sesame oil over it.
7. Stir and serve.
8. You can serve noodles separately in two bowls with the mixture on top of the noodles.

Beijing Egg and Tomato Noodle Soup

Cooking Time: 15 minutes

Serving Size: 2

Calories: 479

Ingredients:

- 1 tablespoon vegetable bouillon powder
- 300g cooked rice noodles (150g uncooked)
- 250g tomatoes (cored and quartered)
- 100g Chinese cabbage (cut into slices)
- 1 tablespoon sesame oil
- 1 tablespoon light soy sauce
- A pinch of white pepper
- 1 egg (beaten)
- 2 spring onions (sliced, to garnish)
- 1 root ginger (peeled and grated)
- 5 fresh shiitake mushrooms (dried and cut into slices)

Method:

1. Heat wok and add ginger, garlic, mushrooms, vegetable powder, and tomatoes.
2. Add 1-liter water in the wok and bring to boil.
3. Cook for 2 minutes until vegetables get softened.
4. Reduce heat to medium and add rice noodles. Add soy sauce and sesame oil.
5. Add remaining ingredients and stir.
6. Add beaten eggs and stir continuously for 2 minutes.
7. Immediately remove from heat and serve.

Radish in Black Rice Vinegar with Crabmeat and Black Sesame Seeds

Cooking Time: 10 minutes

Serving Size: 2

Calories: 333

Ingredients:

- 1 teaspoon rapeseed oil
- 5g black sesame seed (garnish)
- Dried chili flakes (garnish)
- 200g radishes (cut into slices)
- 1 tablespoon black rice vinegar
- 300g radish leaves
- A pinch of caster sugar
- 200g fresh white crab meat

Method:

1. Heat wok on high flame and add the rapeseed oil. Wait for 30 seconds.
2. Add radish sliced and radish leaves in the wok.
3. Stir and add water on the edges of the wok to make steam.
4. Cook for 10 seconds and add remaining ingredients.
5. Remove from heat and serve in a separate dish.
6. Garnish chili flakes and sesame seed on top of the radish.

Lobster Tails, Baby Asparagus and Eggs in Hot Bean Sauce

Cooking Time: 15 minutes

Serving Size: 2

Calories: 230

Ingredients:

- 1 teaspoon corn flour
- 2 spring onions
- 100ml hot vegetable stock
- 1 egg (beaten)
- 1 tablespoon rapeseed oil
- 2 garlic cloves (chopped)
- 200g cooked fresh lobster (sliced into cubes)
- 100g baby asparagus spears
- 1 teaspoon yellow bean paste
- ½ teaspoon dark soy sauce
- 1 tablespoon light soy sauce
- 1 ginger (peeled and grated)
- 1 red chili (chopped)

Method:

1. Heat wok on high flame and add the rapeseed oil. Toss for 5 minutes.
2. Add ginger, garlic, and chili and stir for 2 minutes to release flavor.
3. Add lobsters and stir for 1 minute. Add asparagus and toss for 1 minute more.
4. Add 1 tablespoon water on the edges of the wok to give steam.
5. Add light and dark soy sauce. Stir and add yellow bean paste.
6. Add egg and bring it to boil.

7. Mix the corn flour into 2 tablespoon water and add it into the wok.

8. Stir continuously until thickens.

9. Garnish with onions and serve immediately.

Pineapple Chicken

Cooking Time: 12 minutes

Serving Size: 2

Calories: 240.4

Ingredients:

- A pinch of black pepper
- 1 tablespoon corn flour
- ½ small pineapple (cubes)
- fresh coriander leaves (to garnish)
- 1 tablespoon rapeseed oil
- ½ red pepper (cubes)
- 250g boneless chicken thighs (sliced into cubes)
- sea salt flakes
- 1 spring onion (sliced)
- 2 dried chilies
- roasted cashew nuts

For the Sauce

- 1 teaspoon honey
- ¼ teaspoon Sriracha chili sauce
- 1 tablespoon corn flour
- 100ml pineapple juice

- 1 tablespoon light soy sauce
- 1 lime juice

Method:

1. Take a large bowl and add chicken. Sprinkle pepper and salt. Add corn flour and mix to combine. Set aside.

2. Take all ingredients of the sauce and mix it in a blender. Set aside.

3. Heat a wok on high flame and add the rapeseed oil.

4. Add red chili and stir for flavor.

5. Add chicken pieces and toss for 5 minutes.

6. Add red pepper and pineapple. Cook for 30 seconds.

7. Add sauce and cook until sticky.

8. Add remaining ingredients and cook for 2 minutes more.

9. Remove from flame and garnish with coriander leaves.

Buddha's Stir-Fried Mixed Vegetables

Cooking Time: 15 minutes

Serving Size: 2

Calories: 500

Ingredients:

- 1 tablespoon rapeseed oil
- Ginger root (peeled and grated)
- 4 fresh shiitake mushrooms (dried and sliced)
- 1 cup dried wood ear mushrooms
- 1 cup of fresh beansprouts
- 1 medium carrot

- 1 cup of baby sweetcorn
- ½ teaspoon salted black beans (crushed with rice vinegar 1 tablespoon)
- 1 can of bamboo shoots
- 2 spring onions (garnish)

For the sauce

- 1 tablespoon light soy sauce
- 1 tablespoon vegetarian mushroom sauce
- 100 ml cold vegetable stock
- 1 teaspoon toasted sesame oil
- 1 tablespoon corn flour

Method:

1. Mix all ingredients of sauce in a blender and blend until smooth. Set aside.
2. Heat a wok on high flame and add the rapeseed oil.
3. Add ginger and fry on low heat. Add beans paste and cook for 1 minute.
4. Add vegetables and remaining ingredients except for beansprout. Whisk well.
5. Add sauce and cook for 5 minutes until sticky.
6. Add beansprout and heat for 30 seconds.
7. Transfer to a dish and garnish with onion.

Penang Curry with Chicken

Cooking Time: 35 minutes

Serving Size: 4

Calories: 596

Ingredients:

- 2 peppers fresh red chili peppers
- ¼ cup fresh basil leaves
- 2 tablespoons palm sugar
- 4 cups of coconut milk
- ⅔ pound skinless (boneless and cubed)
- 2 tablespoons fish sauce
- 5 tablespoons Penang curry paste
- cooking oil
- 6 leaf kaffir lime leaves

Method:

1. Heat wok on high flame and add the rapeseed oil.
2. Add curry paste and stir for 2 minutes.
3. Add coconut milk and wait until boiling.
4. Add chicken pieces and cook for 15 minutes.
5. Add remaining ingredients and stir for 2 minutes.
6. Garnish with basil leaves.

Thai Spicy Basil Chicken Fried Rice

Cooking Time: 40 minutes

Serving Size: 6

Calories: 794.1

Ingredients:

- 1 teaspoon white sugar
- ½ cup cilantro sprigs
- 2 peppers serrano peppers (crushed)

- 1 onion (sliced)
- 2 cups sweet basil
- 1-pound boneless chicken breast
- ½ cup sesame oil for frying
- 5 cups jasmine rice (cooked)
- 6 garlic clove (crushed)
- 1 cucumber (sliced)
- 3 tablespoons oyster sauce
- 2 tablespoons fish sauce
- 2 red pepper (sliced)

Method:

1. Take a bowl and mix fish sauce, sugar, and oyster sauce.
2. Heat wok on high flame and add the rapeseed oil.
3. Add serrano pepper and garlic. Stir for 1 minute.
4. Add chicken and sauce mixture. Cook for 5 minutes.
5. Add remaining ingredients except for rice and cook for 10 minutes.
6. Add rice and stir continuously to prevent sticking.
7. Remove from flame and garnish with coriander leaves.

Chinese Buffet Green Beans

Cooking Time: 25 minutes

Serving Size: 6

Calories: 54.5

Ingredients:

- 1-pound fresh green beans (trimmed)
- 2 tablespoons oyster sauce
- 2 teaspoons soy sauce
- 1 tablespoon oil sesame
- 2 cloves garlic (sliced)
- 1 tablespoon white sugar

Method:

1. Heat wok on high flame and add sesame oil.
2. Add garlic and white sugar. Heat until brown.
3. Add green beans and remaining ingredients.
4. Bring to boil and cook for 15 minutes until beans are softened.
5. Garnish with sesame seed and serve.

Summer Special Shrimp and Fruit Fried Rice

Cooking Time: 60 minutes

Serving Size: 2

Calories: 590.8

Ingredients:

- 6 halves walnuts
- 2 cups cold, cooked white rice
- 2 large eggs (beaten)
- 1 tablespoon vegetable oil
- 1 piece of ginger root
- 1 tablespoon soy sauce
- 2 tablespoons cilantro

- ⅔ cup fresh pineapple
- 2 red onions
- 3 green chili peppers
- ½ cup orange segments
- ½ pound shrimp
- salt and pepper

Method:

1. Heat wok on medium flame and add 1 tablespoon oil.
2. Add onion and stir until brown. Set aside.
3. Heat wok on high flame and add shrimp.
4. Stir continuously for 10 minutes until no longer pink in color. Set aside.
5. Wipe wok and heat on high flame. Add ginger, onion, and garlic in 1 tablespoon oil.
6. Stir and heat for 3 minutes until brown on edges.
7. Add pineapple and orange. Stir until pineapple becomes hot.
8. Add remaining ingredients and stir. Add shrimp and onion. Stir for 3 minutes.
9. Garnish with cilantro and serve.

6.2 World Renowned Chinese Recipes

Sichuan Hot Pot

Cooking Time: 1 hour 10 minutes

Serving Size: 1 hot pot

Calories: 259

Ingredients:

For Soup Base:

- 12-14 cups chicken stock
- 10 cloves garlic
- 1 cinnamon stick
- 2 tablespoons oil
- 10 cloves
- 1 tablespoon Sichuan peppercorns
- 10 whole red chilies
- 6 slices ginger
- 3-4 bay leaves
- 1 package spicy hot pot soup base
- 5-star anise

For Dipping Sauce

- Sesame seeds
- Peanuts
- Sesame paste
- Sesame oil
- Cilantro
- Soy sauce
- Chinese black vinegar
- Scallions
- Sacha sauce
- Chili oil
- Garlic

Hot Pot Sides:

- Thinly shaved beef
- Sliced chicken
- Prepared frozen dumplings
- Chinese rice cakes
- Fresh noodles
- Bok choy
- Assorted fish balls
- Thinly sliced fish fillets
- Napa cabbage
- Shiitake mushrooms
- Tofu sheets
- Glass noodles
- Firm tofu
- Soy puffs
- Straw mushrooms
- Green leaf lettuce
- Wood ear mushrooms

Method:

1. To make soup, heat wok and add 1 tablespoon oil and ginger.
2. Stir for 2 minutes. Add garlic, bay leaves, cinnamon stick, cloves, and star anise.
3. Cook for 5 minutes for flavors.
4. Add hot pot soup base, chilies, and peppercorn. Cook for another 2 minutes.

5. Add chicken stock and wait until it starts boiling. Transfer to a broad and deep pot. Set aside

6. Mix all ingredients of dipping sauce and blend until smooth. Set aside.

7. Prepare a hot plate and plugin. Add broth and bring to boil.

8. Pour hot pot side ingredients that you like to add and cook until boil.

9. Place dipping sauce and soup. Serve in the pot.

Braised Pork Ball in Gravy

Cooking Time: 15 minutes

Serving Size: 4

Calories: 684.6

Ingredients:

For meatballs:

- 1 teaspoon salt
- 1 tablespoon dark soy sauce
- 100-gram corn starch
- 1000-gram pork
- 1 leftover steamed bun
- scallion 20 grams
- 2 tablespoon light soy sauce
- 2 tablespoon Shaoxing wine
- 1 cup oil
- 2-gram ginger

For Sauce:

- Sugar ¼ tablespoon
- Corn starch 1 tablespoon
- Dark soy sauce ¼ tablespoon
- 2 slices fresh ginger
- Light soy sauce ½ tablespoon
- Water 1 cup

Method:

1. Add meatball ingredients in a pan and stir continuously in one direction for 5 minutes.
2. Make small round meatballs and set aside.
3. Take all ingredients of the sauce and mix it in a wok or pan.
4. Add oil and stir for 10 minutes.
5. Add meatballs and cook for 30 seconds.
6. Serve hot with rice.

Steamed Garlic Prawns with Vermicelli

Cooking Time: 17 minutes

Serving Size: 2

Calories: 143

Ingredients:

- 10 tiger prawns
- 2 tablespoon light soy sauce
- ¼ teaspoon sugar
- 1 tablespoon cooking oil
- 100 g mung bean vermicelli noodles

- 1 tablespoon water
- 2 tablespoon minced garlic
- 2 tablespoon chopped fresh chili
- 1 tablespoon Shaoxing rice wine
- ¼ teaspoon white pepper
- 1 pinch salt
- scallions for garnishing

Method:

1. Soak noodles and add 1 tablespoon oil to avoid sticking. Set aside.
2. Cut and peel prawns. Put them on noodles.
3. Heat the pan and add oil. Add garlic, water, chili, white pepper, rice wine, soy sauce, and sugar. Heat for 5 minutes until flavored.
4. Add sauce over prawns and noodles.
5. Steam for 5 minutes and serve hot.

Peking Duck

Cooking Time: 1 hour 35 minutes

Serving Size: 4

Calories: 555.7

Ingredients:

- ¼ teaspoon white pepper
- ⅛ teaspoon cloves
- ½ cup plum jam
- 3 tablespoons soy sauce
- 1 tablespoon honey

- 5 green onions
- 1 orange
- 1 tablespoon parsley
- 1 whole duck
- ½ teaspoon cinnamon
- ½ teaspoon ginger
- ¼ teaspoon nutmeg
- 1 ½ teaspoons sugar
- 1 ½ teaspoon white vinegar

Method:

1. Wash duck from inner side and outer side.
2. Mix cinnamon, white pepper, ginger, nutmeg, and cloves.
3. Sprinkle spices mixture on the duck.
4. Add 1 tablespoon vinegar and pour it on the duck.
5. Spread with hands and refrigerate for at least 2 hours.
6. Take a wok and add water. Steam duck from the breast side for 1 hour.
7. Pour lime juice and green onions.
8. Heat oven at 375°F.
9. Remove the skin of the duck and put it in the pan to roast.
10. Roast for 30 minutes. Mix honey with 3 tablespoon soy sauce.
11. Brush it on duck and roast for more than 10 minutes.
12. Mix sugar, chutney, and vinegar to make the sauce.

13. Garnish with parsley and orange slices.

Shrimp Rice Noodle Rolls

Cooking Time: 15 minutes

Serving Size: 8

Calories: 118

Ingredients:

For Shrimp:

- ½ teaspoon sugar
- ¼ teaspoon baking soda
- 2 tablespoons water
- ½ teaspoon cornstarch
- ¼ teaspoon sesame oil
- ¼ teaspoon salt
- 8 ounces shrimp
- ¼ teaspoon white pepper

For Sauce:

- 1 teaspoon oyster sauce
- 1 teaspoon oil
- 2 teaspoons dark soy sauce
- 5 teaspoons sugar
- 1 scallion
- 6 slices ginger
- 2 ½ tablespoons light soy sauce
- ¼ cup of water
- Salt

For the Rice Noodle Rolls:

- 1 cup of water
- Vegetable or canola oil
- 5 tablespoons rice flour
- 1 tablespoon mung bean starch
- 2 tablespoons wheat starch
- 2 tablespoons cornstarch
- ¼ teaspoon salt

Method:

1. Coat shrimps with baking soda, sugar, and water.
2. Refrigerate for 2 hours and wash thoroughly.
3. Coat shrimp with white pepper, sesame oil, cornstarch, and salt.
4. Cover and refrigerate for 1 hour.
5. Mix all ingredients of sauce and heat on low flame.
6. Cook until smooth.
7. Wet a clean cloth and set aside.
8. Steam shrimps for 10 minutes and put in a bowl.
9. Add rice noodles and add shrimps.
10. Cover with wet cloth and roll.
11. Remove the cloth and cut rice noodles lengthwise.
12. Serve with sauce.

Mapo Tofu

Cooking Time: 35 minutes

Serving Size: 6

Calories: 335

Ingredients:

- ¼ teaspoon sugar
- 6-8 dried red chilies
- 1 ½ tablespoon Sichuan peppercorns
- 3 tablespoons ginger
- 3 tablespoons garlic
- ¼ cup low sodium chicken broth
- 1-pound silken tofu
- 1 scallion
- ½ cup oil
- 1-2 fresh chili peppers
- 1 ½ teaspoons cornstarch
- ¼ teaspoon sesame oil
- 8 ounces pork
- 1-2 tablespoons spicy bean sauce

Method:

1. Heat wok and add chilies in oil. Stir for 5 minutes for the fragment. Set aside.
2. Heat wok and add oil. Add peppercorn, garlic, and ginger. Cook for 7 minutes.
3. Add ground pork and cook until pink color disappears.
4. Add bean mixture and chicken broth. Stir well.
5. Add water in cornstarch. Mix and add into bean mixture.
6. Add remaining ingredients and seasonings. Stir for 10 minutes.

7. Serve hot and garnish with onion.

Yang Chow Fried Rice

Cooking Time: 35 minutes

Serving Size: 6

Calories: 301

Ingredients:

- 2 teaspoons salt
- 10 pieces shrimps
- 1 teaspoon garlic
- 3 tablespoons cooking oil
- ¼ cup green onion
- 2 pieces of raw eggs beaten
- 1 teaspoon sugar
- 6 cups cooked white rice
- 1 cup barbecued pork
- 1 ½ tablespoons soy sauce
- ¾ cup green peas
- 1 teaspoon ginger

Method:

1. Take a pan and heat garlic and ginger in oil.
2. Add shrimps and cook for 5 minutes. Set aside.
3. Add eggs and stir for 30 seconds.
4. Add rice in egg and mix thoroughly.
5. Add sauce, sugar, and other spices.
6. Add barbecue pork and cook for 5 minutes.

7. Add shrimp and green peas. Cook for 5 minutes.

8. Add green onions and cook for 1 minute.

9. Transfer to plate and serve.

Wonton Soup

Cooking Time: 40 minutes

Serving Size: 6

Calories: 289.6

Ingredients:

- 2 bok choy
- 2 cloves garlic
- 1 tablespoon ginger
- 4 cups chicken broth
- 3 green onions
- 1 tablespoon sesame oil
- 4 ounces shiitake mushrooms
- 1 tablespoon yellow miso paste

For Wontons

- 1 tablespoon reduced-sodium soy sauce
- 1 tablespoon ginger
- 1 tablespoon oyster sauce
- 1 teaspoon sesame oil
- 8 ounces medium shrimp
- 2 cloves garlic
- 2 green onions
- ½ teaspoon Sriracha

- ¼ teaspoon black pepper
- 36 wonton wrappers

Method:

1. Take a large bowl and combine garlic, ginger, shrimp, Sriracha, soy sauce, sesame oil, and oyster sauce.
2. Put wonton wrappers and pour 1 tablespoon shrimp mixture over it.
3. Fold wrappers and press edges to seal.
4. Take a pan and heat on low flame.
5. Add garlic, ginger, and chicken broth.
6. Add 2 cups water and bring to boil.
7. Add mushrooms and cook for 10 minutes.
8. Add green onions, bok choy, miso paste, and cook for 3 minutes.
9. Add wonton and stir for 2 minutes.
10. Serve hot with sauce.

Chinese Egg Fried Rice

Cooking Time: 20 minutes

Serving Size: 2

Calories: 163

Ingredients:

- 1 big onion diced
- 3 eggs beaten
- 2 spring onion
- 3 tablespoon vegetable oil
- 3 cups cooked rice

Seasonings:

- 2 tablespoon light soy sauce
- 1 teaspoon salt
- ½ teaspoon ground white pepper

Method:

1. Beat eggs and cut vegetables.
2. Heat a wok on high flame and add 1 tablespoon oil.
3. Add eggs and stir continuously.
4. Remove eggs from heat and set aside.
5. Heat wok again and add 1 tablespoon oil.
6. Add eggs and stir immediately. Do not burn the rice.
7. Add vegetables and salt, pepper.
8. Mix again and add soy sauce from the edges of the wok.
9. Cook for 2 minutes and serve hot with parsley and onion garnishing.

French Onion Rice

Cooking Time: 1 hour 30 minutes

Serving Size: 8

Calories: 135

Ingredients:

- 2 cup basmati rice
- 3 cup low-sodium beef broth
- 1 tablespoon thyme leaves
- 1 teaspoon freshly ground black pepper
- ¼ white wine

- 6 cloves garlic, minced
- Lemon wedges
- 6 tablespoon butter
- 1 tablespoon olive oil
- 2 large onions
- 1 ¼ teaspoon kosher salt

Method:

1. Take a large pan and heat. Add butter and onion.
2. Add salt and cook for 30 minutes until caramelized. Set aside.
3. Take a pan and add 1 tablespoon oil.
4. Add rice, garlic thyme, and lemon, wine, and stir well.
5. Add caramelized mixture ¾ and seasoning in rice. Combine and cook for 3 minutes.
6. Add broth and wait to boil.
7. Reduce heat and cook for 15 minutes.
8. Transfer to bowl and add remaining caramelized mixture. Garnish with thyme.

6.3 Recipes of Vegetarian Chinese Meals

15-Minute Garlic Noodles

Cooking Time: 15 minutes

Serving Size: 3

Calories: 426

Ingredients:

- 4 green onions

- 4 tablespoons peanut oil
- 2 teaspoon ginger
- 1 bell pepper
- 4 cloves garlic
- 6 oz. Chow Mein noodles

Sauce:

- 1 tablespoon soy sauce
- ½ teaspoon sesame oil
- ¼ cup chicken broth
- 2 tablespoons Shaoxing wine
- 2 tablespoons oyster sauce

Method:

1. Take a bowl and mix all ingredients of sauce until smooth.
2. Cook noodles by following directions on the package. Rinse with water and add 1 tablespoon oil to prevent sticking.
3. Add oil in a wok or pan and add noodles.
4. Stir noodles to prevent sticking to the wok.
5. Add vegetables and stir for 3 minutes.
6. Add sauce and mix well.
7. Cook for 1 minute and serve immediately.

General Tso Tofu

Cooking Time: 30 minutes

Serving Size: 3

Calories: 345

Ingredients:

- 1 tablespoon maple syrup
- 6 tablespoons cornstarch
- 1 block tofu
- 2 tablespoons soy sauce

Sauce:

- 2 teaspoons cornstarch
- 2 tablespoons Shaoxing wine
- ¼ cup chicken stock
- 2 tablespoons Chinkiang vinegar
- ¼ cup of sugar
- 1 tablespoon light soy sauce
- 1 tablespoon dark soy sauce

Stir fry:

- 2 teaspoons ginger
- 3 to 4 cloves garlic
- 3 tablespoons peanut oil
- 4 green onions
- 2 fresh Thai chili pepper
- 2 bunches broccoli

Method:

1. Marinate tofu with maple syrup and soy sauce in a sealing bag for 10 to 15 minutes.
2. Mix all ingredients of the sauce and stir until combine properly.

3. Gently open the bag of tofu and discard extra liquid. Add cornstarch and mix tofu well.

4. Heat wok and add 1 tablespoon oil.

5. Add broccoli and 3 tablespoon water. Cover immediately to cook broccoli in steam. Heat for 4 minutes and set aside.

6. Clean wok and add 1 tablespoon oil.

7. Add tofu in the wok and cook for 10 minutes until brown. Set aside.

8. Add remaining ingredients in wok and stir well until sauce becomes thick.

9. Transfer tofu on the plate. Pour broccoli and sauce. Serve with rice.

Nepali Momus with Spinach and Ricotta

Cooking Time: 50 minutes

Serving Size: 20

Calories: 75

Ingredients:

- ¼ cup parmesan cheese
- 2 green onions
- 20 round dumplings wrappers
- ¾ cup ricotta cheese
- 5 cups spinach leaves
- 1 clove garlic
- Freshly ground black pepper
- 1 tablespoon butter
- ¾ teaspoon salt

Method:

1. Take a skillet and add spinach and garlic. Add 3 tablespoon water and cook for 5 minutes until spinach wilted. Set aside.

2. Mix all ingredients except dumpling wraps.

3. Add 1 tablespoon mixture in each dumpling and wrap like half-moon shape.

4. Steam dumplings for 10 minutes until cook. Serve with sauce.

Real Deal Sesame Noodles

Cooking Time: 20 minutes

Serving Size: 4

Calories: 166

Ingredients:

- 2 green onions
- 250 grams of noodles

Peanut sauce:

- 2 cloves garlic
- ¼ teaspoon Sichuan peppercorn powder
- 2 tablespoons light soy sauce
- 2 tablespoons Chinkiang vinegar
- 1 tablespoon honey
- ¼ cup natural peanut butter
- 2 teaspoons chili oil
- 1 teaspoon sesame oil
- 1 teaspoon ginger

Topping options:

- tomatoes

- sesame seeds

- 1 cucumber

- 2 carrots

Method:

1. Cook noodles by following package directions. Rinse and add 1 tablespoon oil to prevent sticking.

2. Add peanut butter in warm water and make a smooth paste.

3. Add remaining ingredients and cook for 5 minutes until thick sauce forms.

4. Add noodles in a pan and add the sauce. Mix well. Garnish with sesame seeds and cucumber.

Homemade Vegetarian Oyster Sauce

Cooking Time: 20 minutes

Serving Size: 1

Calories: 40

Ingredients:

- 1 tablespoon dark soy sauce

- 1 teaspoon ginger

- 1 tablespoon light soy sauce

- 1 teaspoon agave syrup

- 2 teaspoons miso paste

- 1.4 oz. shiitake mushrooms

- 2 tablespoons peanut oil

- ¼ teaspoon five-spice powder
- 2 teaspoons sesame oil
- 2 cloves garlic

Method:

1. Wash shiitake mushroom and add hot water in it. Wait for 30 minutes until mushroom tender.
2. Dry mushrooms and cut into small pieces.
3. Take a wok and fry mushrooms in 1 tablespoon oil. Cook for 5 minutes.
4. Add ginger garlic and cook for 1 minute.
5. Add 1 cup of water in the blender and blend the mushroom mixture.
6. Transfer to the frying pan and add remaining ingredients. Add seasonings to taste and cook for 10 minutes.
7. Cooldown and store in a container for 1 week or refrigerator for 1 month.

Carrot Dumplings

Cooking Time: 20

Serving Size: 45 minutes

Calories: 38

Ingredients:

- 45 dumpling wrappers
- 2 teaspoons potato starch

Filling:

- 4 cloves garlic
- 1 tablespoon light soy sauce
- ½ teaspoon salt
- 1-pound carrots
- 3 large eggs
- 1 cup bamboo shoots
- 1 cup shiitake mushrooms
- 2 slices ginger
- 3 tablespoons sesame oil
- ¼ teaspoon white pepper powder

Sauce:

- 2 teaspoons light soy sauce
- 2 tablespoons black vinegar
- 2 teaspoons chili oil

Method:

1. Wash shiitake mushroom and add hot water in it. Wait for 30 minutes until mushroom tender.
2. Dry mushrooms and cut into small pieces.
3. Take a wok and fry mushrooms in 1 tablespoon oil. Cook for 5 minutes.
4. Add ginger, garlic, and carrot and cook for 1 minute.
5. Add 1 cup of water in the blender and blend the mushroom mixture.
6. Transfer to pan and cook until carrots soften. Add eggs and cook for 2 minutes.

7. Add soy sauce, bamboo shoots, salt, and white pepper. Mix and set aside.

8. Combine potato starch with water and brush on dumpling wraps.

9. Add 1 tablespoon mixture overwraps and seal dumplings.

10. Mix all ingredients of the sauce and stir until combine.

11. Steam dumplings for 8 to 10 minutes and serve with sauce.

Di San Xian

Cooking Time: 30 minutes

Serving Size: 2

Calories: 220

Ingredients:

- ½ tablespoon dark soy sauce
- 1 tablespoon Shaoxing wine
- ¼ cup vegetable stock
- ½ tablespoon sugar
- ¼ teaspoon salt
- 1 teaspoon cornstarch
- 1 tablespoon light soy sauce

Stir fry:

- 1 bell pepper
- 2 teaspoons sesame seeds for garnish
- ½ regular eggplant
- 2 green onion

- 2 cloves of garlic
- 2 teaspoons cornstarch
- ¼ cup peanut oil
- 1 small russet potato

Method:

1. Soak eggplants in water for 15 to 20 minutes and sprinkle salt over it.
2. Cut eggplant in small pieces and sprinkle cornstarch.
3. Mix cornstarch, salt, soy sauce, oil, and wine. Set aside.
4. Heat a skillet and add oil. Cook eggplants until golden brown.
5. Remove eggplant and add potato pieces in the skillet.
6. Add garlic and onion and stir fry.
7. Mix sauce until thicken.
8. Add remaining ingredients and eggplants. Mix and serve immediately.

Chinese Broccoli

Cooking Time: 20 minutes

Serving Size: 4

Calories: 90

Ingredients:

- 4 cloves garlic
- 1 bunch Chinese broccoli
- Pinch of salt
- ½ lb. white mushrooms
- 1 tablespoon peanut oil

Sauce:

- 1 tablespoon cornstarch
- 2 tablespoons soy sauce
- 1 cup vegetable stock
- 2 teaspoons sugar
- 1 teaspoon dark soy sauce

Method:

1. Mix all sauce ingredients and set aside.
2. Take a wok and add water. Add broccoli and steam for 5 minutes.
3. Remove excess water and add oil and garlic.
4. Cook for 3 minutes. Add mushroom until golden brown.
5. Add remaining ingredients and sauce. Cook for 2 minutes and serve.

Chinese Banana Fritters

Cooking Time: 25 minutes

Serving Size: 6

Calories: 196

Ingredients:

- Oil for deep frying
- Powdered sugar
- 5 big ripe bananas

Batter

- 1 tablespoon granulated sugar
- ½ cup cornstarch

- 2 tablespoons milk
- ½ cup all-purpose flour
- 1 tablespoon butter
- ½ cup of water

Method:

1. Combine all ingredients of batter and mix until smooth.
2. Heat oil in the pan. Add banana slices in batter and pour in hot oil.
3. Cook for 5 minutes until golden brown.
4. Serve with sugar or maple syrup.

Mango Sago

Cooking Time: 30 minutes

Serving Size: 4

Calories: 340

Ingredients:

- 1 cup full-fat coconut milk
- 2 big mangoes
- ¾ cup evaporated milk
- ½ grapefruit
- ¼ cup tapioca pearls
- ¼ cup of sugar

Method:

1. Boil water and add tapioca pearls until transparent. Add in sieve and merge with tapioca pearls. Set aside
2. Blend half mangoes in milk to make a smooth mixture. Add sugar and blend again.

3. Take a bowl and add tapioca pearls. Add mango paste and coconut oil. Garnish with mango slices.

Conclusion

Chinese foods are very different from all other foods in different countries. Ingredients and taste can vary from region to region in China too, but their preparation method is almost identical. Chinese foods have been prevailing since ancient times and are widely famous for their unique taste and healthy ingredients. There are many benefits of eating Chinese food as it provides nutrients that a body needs and it also uses fewer fat ingredients. Rice is the leading food item in China that is served with every dish and in every meal. Buddhists who cannot consume meat can eat vegetarian dishes. The basic techniques of Chinese food are frying, deep-frying, steaming, boiling, and roasting. Chinese food made at home is very different from the food available at restaurants. There are many health benefits to consuming Chinese food. It helps to regulate your body fluids and enhance your metabolism. Thus, Chinese food is famous in America for its flavors and cooking styles. Vegetarians, lacto-Ovo-vegetarians, Buddhists, Ovo-vegetarians, etc., all can eat Chinese foods due to a wide variety of cooking techniques.

Printed in Great Britain
by Amazon